RE-IMAGINING BENGAL
architecture, built environment and cultural heritage

RE-IMAGINING BENGAL
architecture, built environment and cultural heritage

edited by
Iftekhar Ahmed, Mohammad Habib Reza

RE-IMAGINING BENGAL
architecture, built environment and cultural heritage

Iftekhar Ahmed, Mohammad Habib Reza **Eds.**

First edition 2018 published by Copal Publishers
© Copal Publishing Group, 2018

All rights reserved. No part of this publication may be reproduced, distributed, or transmitted in any form or by any means, including photocopying, recording, or other electronic or mechanical methods, without the prior written permission of the publisher, except in the case of brief quotations embodied in critical reviews and certain other noncommercial uses permitted by copyright law.

Cover design
MOHAMMAD HABIB REZA

Cover sketch
SAJID BIN DOZA

Graphic Design
MOHAMMAD HABIB REZA
IFTEKHAR AHMED

ISBN: 978-93-83419-64-7 (Print)
ISBN: 978-93-83419-65-4 (e-book)

Published by

COPAL PUBLISHING GROUP
E-143, Lajpat Nagar, Sahibabad,
Dist: Ghaziabad, UP - 201005. India
www.copalpublisbing.com

TABLE OF CONTENTS

	Preface	v
	List of figures and tables	vi
	Short biography of contributors	viii

CHAPTER 1   RE-IMAGINING BENGAL: CRITICAL THOUGHTS   1
Mohammad Habib Reza, Iftekhar Ahmed

CHAPTER 2   RETHINKING THE POST-GUPTA BENGAL: SETTLEMENT AND   17
ARCHITECTURE
Mohammad Habib Reza

CHAPTER 3   PUNDRANAGAR: THE OTHER STORY OF A MEDIEVAL   33
WALLED CITY OF GAUR
Sajid Bin Doza

CHAPTER 4   LEARNING FROM PANAM NAGAR: LESSONS FROM THE   53
TRANSITIONAL BRITISH COLONIAL HYBRID HOUSES
Iftekhar Ahmed, Badruzzahan Ahmed

CHAPTER 5   SOCIAL CAPITAL IN PARTICIPATORY INFORMAL HERITAGE   77
MANAGEMENT: CASES FROM OLD DHAKA
Iftekhar Ahmed

CHAPTER 6   A COMMUNITY-INVOLVED STRATEGIC MANAGEMENT PLAN   107
FOR CHHOTO KATRA
Mohammad Habib Reza, Iftekhar Ahmed

PREFACE

The book owes its existence to one simple stimulus: lack of enough materials on the architecture, built environment and cultural heritage of Bengal. The existing ones offer scarce in-depth analysis, where many of them simply describe the subject area on surface, highly influenced by misinterpretations and myths. A fresh perspective has been long due to cope with the complicacies of contemporary thoughts, philosophical development and recent discoveries through excavations.

The initial idea of the book was to cover a broader spectrum of subject matters with a possibility of contributions from the experts of various fields closely related to Bengal. However, through the editorial process towards a theme-based compilation, the current content of the book gradually evolved and ultimately the selected chapters came under a more focused stream. The remaining task was to decide how to present the materials in a reasonably concise and readable manner which was achieved by arranging the chapters in a sequence of revisiting history, architectural history and study of heritage management.

Aim of this book is to spot light on a segment of the large diaspora of knowledge that the region offers. It should be noted that in individual fields there have almost always been greater experts and varying opinions; this book is no exception where a group of authors are offering their views based on their expertise. This compilation intrigues many questions, of which only a few are within the scope of this book to answer. However, there is no doubt that it will spark further investigation. When it does, perhaps this will be the contribution of this effort in its small way. Rather than going for conventional narratives, the works focus on in-depth analysis to explore new areas of knowledge in architecture, built environment and cultural heritage of Bengal.

Iftekhar Ahmed
Mohammad Habib Reza

LIST OF FIGURES

Figure 1.1	Map of Bengal showing ancient kingdoms	xii
Figure 1.2	Mausoleum of Chhoto Katra	3
Figure 1.3	Shatgumbad Mosque	5
Figure 1.4	Paharpur Mahāvihāra	6
Figure 1.5	Panam Nagar	8
Figure 1.6	Improper restoration at Panam Nagar	9
Figure 2.1	Conjectural reconstruction of the early cruciform shrine of post-Gupta Bengal	16
Figure 2.2	Early Gupta shrine	18
Figure 2.3	Bengal during the post-Gupta period	19
Figure 2.4	Early settlement pattern of Bengal	25
Figure 2.5	Early post-Gupta shrine	26
Figure 2.6	Cruciform shrine of Bengal	26
Figure 2.7	Incorporation of crown to the shrine	27
Figure 2.8	Development of cruciform shrine	28
Figure 3.1	Gumti gate	32
Figure 3.2	Bengal and Assam in the ninteenth century	34
Figure 3.3	Bengal in the seventeenth century	35
Figure 3.4	Fortified walls of Gaur	36
Figure 3.5	Ancient paintings of Gaur	37
Figure 3.6	Painting of Chhoto Shona mosque, Gaur	38
Figure 3.7	Flow chart of different spatial organization	39
Figure 3.8	Evolution of Sultanate Gaur	40
Figure 3.9	Ruins of inland port area at Phulbari	41
Figure 3.10	Mohallah of Sultanate Capital of Gaur	43
Figure 3.11	Spatial relationship of tank with adjacent functions	44
Figure 3.12	Ornamental tiles of Gaur	46
Figure 3.14	Diagrammatic analysis showing hierarchy of spaces	47
Figure 4.1	Exterior of House 5	52
Figure 4.2	Street front houses of Panam Nagar	54
Figure 4.3	Plan showing hybrid houses of Panam Nagar	55
Figure 4.4	Plans of House 5 showing various zones and circulation	60
Figure 4.5	Plan of Houses 13-11-9-7 showing various zones and circulation	63
Figure 4.6	Exterior of Houses 13-11-9-7	64
Figure 4.7	Axonometric view of Houses 16-18-20-22 showing layering of space	66

Figure 4.8	Plan of Houses 16-18-20-22 showing various zones and circulation	67
Figure 4.9	Interior of House 16	68
Figure 4.10	Plan of House 38 showing various zones and circulation	70
Figure 4.11	Exterior of House 38	71
Figure 5.1	Verandah of Pogose school	76
Figure 5.2	Aerial views of Old Dhaka showing high density traditional neighborhoods	79
Figure 5.3	Continuity of mahallas showing growth of physical and sociocultural layers	80
Figure 5.4	Tangible and intangible heritage elements of Old Dhaka	81
Figure 5.5	The entrepreneurial social infrastructure model	84
Figure 5.6	Panchayet house and activities in Old Dhaka	87
Figure 5.7	Improper restoration work at Panam Nagar, left: before and right: after	90
Figure 5.8	Chini-tikri work at Kosaituli mosque	94
Figure 5.9	Pogose High School	97
Figure 5.10	Summary of the informal heritage management activities in Old Dhaka	99
Figure 5.11	A possible support system for future of informal heritage management system in Old Dhaka	101
Figure 6.1	The central mausoleum of Chhoto Katra crammed by illegal encroachment	106
Figure 6.2	Buriganga riverbank in 1861 CE	108
Figure 6.4	Charles D'Oyly's sketch of Chhoto Katra	112
Figure 6.5	Chhoto Katra and its surroundings in map of Mughal Dhaka	113
Figure 6.6	Chhoto Katra and its surroundings in 1859 CE	114
Figure 6.7	Three development phases of Chhoto Katra and its surroundings	115
Figure 6.8	Chhoto Katra and its surroundings	116
Figure 6.9	Present state of Chhoto Katra	117

LIST OF TABLES

| Table 5.1 | Key forces and mechanism of informal heritage management process | 92 |
| Table 5.2 | Actions and activities of informal heritage management process | 93 |

SHORT BIOGRAPHY OF CONTRIBUTORS

EDITORS
IFTEKHAR AHMED
Iftekhar Ahmed is trained in Architecture, Urban Design and Heritage Conservation. After receiving Bachelor of Architecture from Bangladesh University of Engineering and Technology in 2001, he worked at URBANA Architectural Consultants, Dhaka, as architect for two years. In 2003, he joined BRAC University as a Lecturer. In 2005, he received the ADB-Japan scholarship to complete Master of Urban Design from the University of Hong Kong. He received his PhD from the Department of Architecture of National University of Singapore in 2012. His area of research was informal heritage management. He worked as a Research Fellow at the Centre for Sustainable Asian Cities, School of Design and Environment, National University of Singapore in projects such as *Benchmarks, Best Practices and Framework for Sustainable Urban Development and Cities*. Currently, he is working at Department of Architecture of BRAC University as Assistant Professor. His research and practice focus on participatory heritage management, affordable housing and sustainable development.

MOHAMMAD HABIB REZA
Mohammad Habib Reza is an architect, architectural historian and heritage management professional, completed his Bachelor of Architecture degree from Khulna University in 2001 and PhD in architectural history and theory from Nottingham Trent University, UK in 2013. His PhD title was *Early Buddhist Architecture of Bengal: Morphological Study on the Vihāras of c. 3rd to 8th centuries*, where he proposes the morphological development pattern of ancient and mediaeval Buddhist architecture of Bengal. He is one of the founder member of the Centre for the Study of Architecture and Cultural Heritage in India, Arabia and the Maghreb (ArCHIAM), presently

based at Liverpool University, UK. He worked for several heritage management projects of traditional oasis settlements in Central Oman funded by the Ministry of Heritage and Culture of Oman. His research interest focuses on the geometric and morphological development of architecture plus settlements and their connection with cultural, social and religious processes. His research further explores the connection between Bengal and other culture and their architectural styles. He was the Principle Investigator for the project titled *Documentation of Islamic Heritage of Bangladesh* funded by the AGA KHAN Development Network. Presently he is an Assistant Professor at Department of Architecture of BRAC University.

OTHER AUTHORS
SAJID BIN DOZA

Sajid Bin Doza is working at the Department of Architecture of BRAC University as Assistant Professor. He did his PhD in Art History & Heritage Study jointly from University of Evora and University of Lisboa, Portugal, in 2016. His PhD title was *Riverine Fortress City of `Mahasthan´ in Deltaic Bengal: In search for the traditional settlement pattern of ancient cities*. Before this he did Master of Architecture from Bangladesh University of Engineering & Technology in 2008, his dissertation was *Analysis and Identification of Spatial Pattern in Rajshahi Old Town*. He did his Bachelor of Architecture in 1999 from Khulna University. Currently, he is exploring the sociocultural trends in the field of architecture by focusing on Bengal's heritage to increase awareness about the region's vigorous past.

BADRUZZAHAN AHMED

Badruzzahan Ahmed is an architect, whose work interests focus on history and cultural heritage. A graduate of Bachelor of Architecture from BRAC University in 2014, she is currently pursuing Master of Architecture at the Melbourne School of Design. She received the Erasmus Mundus Scholarship in 2011–2012 and studied as an exchange student at the Universidade de Evora, Portugal. Previously, she worked at Team Architrave, Chartered Architect in Colombo Sri Lanka and as a Teaching Assistant at the Department of Architecture, BRAC University. She is also a travel writer and her articles have been published in several magazines including Ice Today and Ice Business. Beyond work, her interests include traveling, exploring new cultures, painting and writing.

FIGURE 1.1: Map of Bengal showing ancient kingdoms
The map shows ancient kingdoms of Bengal and its surroundings with present day political boundaries of Bangladesh and West Bengal, India.

Source: Author

RE-IMAGINING BENGAL: CRITICAL THOUGHTS

Mohammad Habib Reza
Iftekhar Ahmed

WHY RE-IMAGINE
The historical narratives of the Indian subcontinent dates back to pre-Ashokan period. Ashokan edicts, in particular, are well acknowledged and understood. These edicts as well as other archaeological findings give glimpse of ancient India. It has been authoritatively estimated that something like eighty percent of our knowledge of the history of India before about c. 1000 CE is derived from inscriptional sources (Salomon, 1998). However, the contemporary practice of writing history cannot be traced back before the British colonial era. The historical sources before this were sporadic, often depending on patronage of a strong ruler. While in other cases they were passed on through oral history. As their nature suggests, this form of history gets deformed, reinterpreted even personalized.

> *The poor condition of the logical analysis of history is shown by the fact that neither historians, nor methodologists of history, but rather representatives of very unrelated disciplines have conducted the authoritative investigations into this important question.*
>
> -Max Weber

Contested narratives of written history need to be re-evaluated with the need of changing time. This happens due to (often) personalized interpretation of history by the historians (Fischer, 1970). Bengal history carries the historians' fallacy in three phases. Firstly, the selective recording of the British historians found to best suit their purpose. Secondly, post-partition (division of Indian subcontinent in 1947 CE) creation of *Syndicated Hinduism* (Thapar, 2010) that frequently suppressed regional events, which still continues today by many historians habitually carrying the 'baggage' left by the past and present a skewed view. Finally, contemporary efforts of historians' *Deconstructing History* (Munslow, 2006) to establish their own identity by offering a constructed view which often deviates from the facts.

These three trends of interpreting history unhappily format the contemporary discourse of many multidisciplinary issues. Two key observations follow: there are parts of history that are not clearly evident while the others, even though documented in cases, actually present skewed interpretation based on their beliefs. It is at this junction that this book aims to offer a different perspective, yet to be fully explored and perhaps in its own way contribute to fill a part of this gap. A critical part of Bengal's history partially got suppressed due to the dominance of Hinduism in historical documentation by a group of historians. This repressed significance of a part of Buddhist era and subsequently many contributions of that time period disappeared into oblivion.

The time between the decline of Guptas (c. 650 CE) and the rise of the magnificent Pala Empire (c. 750 CE) is actually a misinterpretation known as *Matsayana*. This period (late seventh and early eighth century) is acknowledged by the historians as devoid of any cultural development similar to the European dark ages of pre-Renaissance. This phase is seldom discussed except as background for the next phase, the Pala art and architecture. History of Bengal before the Palas is obscure and archaeological evidences from this period are scant, which rather than establishing a distinct style actually aids this misinterpretation. In the history of the Indian subcontinent, this period is marked as the time of de-urbanization and the decline of cultural development. The achievement of the Gupta dynasty is far more celebrated as the classical period of Indian art and architecture with examples of Ajanta and Ellora. Naturally, when the Buddhist Pala dynasty superseded the Hindu Gupta dynasty in this region it was not equally noted. Most accepted counts of history marked the decline of the Guptas above the period before Pala development. This obscure part of history, noted so forth as pre-Pala period, lacks in two major areas: there are rare archaeological evidences of the period and often the ones recorded are credited to later dynasties (Reza, 2008, 2010, 2012; Reza, Bandyopadhyay, & Mowla, 2015).

FIGURE 1.2: Mausoleum of Chhoto Katra
The single dome mausoleum sat on the center of the courtyard, was square in plan with corner turrets with a rectangular platform in the west.

Source: Charles D'Oyly

Spread of Islam in the Indian subcontinent is another highly contested issue. A popular belief is it came here through the blazing swords, known as '*sword theory*' (Banu, 1992), with mass destruction of Hindu temples. Islam began to make headway in Bengal, consequent on and subsequent to the establishment of political Islam and no doubt there were forced conversions. Several established school of thoughts strongly support this view even though the historical evidence suggests otherwise (Eaton, 1993). The total number of temples that were destroyed across those six centuries (from 1000 CE to 1600 CE) was 80, not many thousands as is sometimes conjectured by various people (Eaton, 2004). However Bengal's contact with the Muslims, especially in the field of trade, colonization and missionary work, began much earlier than its conquest in the thirteenth century (Sarkar, 1972). This shows there is scope for ground breaking studies following the footsteps of authors who have already challenged the 'popular beliefs'.

Another uncertain and highly debated (Haque, 2009) fragment of Bengal's history is the origin of Dhaka city which is officially documented as 1608 CE; while archaeological evidence strongly suggests otherwise. This is probably related to approximately four hundred years of rather ambiguous history, starting from the Tughlaq sultanate rulers (forteenth century CE) to the establishment of *Jahangirnagar* (later renamed Dhaka) by Emperor Jahangir, the strong Mughal ruler in the seventeenth century. Archaeological evidence and inscription trace back existence of urban life in Dhaka almost eight hundred years ago when Dhaka was the capital of Iklim or province Mubarakabad (Ahmed, Ali, Alam, & Musa, 2000; Shahnewaz & Haque, 2014). The inscription on domes of Binat Bibi mosque of Narinda, Dhaka, shows it was built by Musammat Bakht Binat, daughter of Marhamat in 1456-57 CE. The inscription is probably the oldest archaeological evidence that supports existence of urban life in Dhaka in the fifteenth century (Begum, 2014).

Tangible heritage are the crystallization of intangible elements (Powell, Lim, & Invernizzi, 1994), which in most traditional settlements are more celebrated for their visible qualities. Comparatively, intangible heritage elements are difficult to decipher through common observation and subsequently require more in-depth investigation and/or clear understanding (Ahmed, 2012). The Venice Charter in 1964 recognized heritage having cultural, architectural, historical, scientific and social significance. It also identified the importance of heritage setting and original fabric, documentation, contribution from all periods in the buildings character, maintenance of heritage for social purpose (ICOMOS, 1964). However the importance of intangible heritage was not recognized and it continued till the declaration of the Nara Document on Authenticity in 1994 (UNESCO, ICCROM, & ICOMOS, 1994). Since the last two decades following Nara, the importance of intangible heritage has been recognized globally. UNESCO's Convention for the Safeguarding of the Intangible Heritage identifies the importance of oral traditions and expressions, including language as a vehicle of the intangible cultural heritage, performing arts, social practices, rituals and festive events, knowledge and practices concerning nature and the universe, and traditional craftsmanship as critical intangible heritage elements (UNESCO, 2003).

Traditional Ainu dance is performed by the indigenous people of Hokkaidō in northern Japan at ceremonies and banquets, as part of newly organized cultural festivals and privately in daily life; in its various forms. The dance form is closely connected to the lifestyle

FIGURE 1.3: Shatgumbad Mosque

The magnificent Sultanate mosque at Khalifatabad is listed as a UNESCO World Heritage Monument. Built by Khan al-Azam Ulugh Khan Jahan in the fifteenth century; it is the largest of the Sultanate mosques in Bangladesh, displaying a unique blend of indigenous elements with the imperial style of Delhi.

Source: Author

and religion of the Ainu. The traditional style involves a large circle of dancers, sometimes with onlookers who sing an accompaniment without musical instrumentation. Recognizing the significance of the dance form and its influence on everyday life of local people, the indigenous Ainu dance has been inscribed by UNESCO in the representative list of the Intangible Cultural Heritage of Humanity in 2009 (UNESCO, 2016d).

With proud examples of intangible heritage elements being marked globally, it is virtually missing in this region. Bengal boasts of having a rich and diverse pool of intangible elements, of which some can be traced back thousands of years. They include cultural practices, local customs and rituals, crafts and arts, language, folklore, legends, attitudes, traditions, the interactions of community and places, among many others. Compared to tangible heritage, being conserved partially at varying capacity, the intangible elements are rarely considered or receive international recognition. Intermittent attempts to document or revive them often fall short. As a result, the list of intangible elements is ever shrinking with regular disappearance due to lack of practice and/or patronage.

Heritage management practices recognized as being successful and sustainable can include everything from involving local people in site management, to creating innovative policies and regulating tourism (UNESCO, 2016c). Charter for the protection and management of the archaeological heritage (1990) includes the responsibilities of public

FIGURE 1.4: Paharpur *Mahāvihāra*
Remains of the seventh to tenth century CE Buddhist monastery of Bengal. One of the masterpieces of the Pala era, the Paharpur Mahāvihāra was the center of culture and administration of this region.

Source: Author

authorities and legislators, principles relating to the professional performance of the processes of inventorisation, survey, excavation, documentation, research, maintenance, conservation, preservation, reconstruction, information, presentation, public access and use of the heritage as essential elements of heritage management (ICAHM, 1990). Following this guideline, there are several good practices in the field of global heritage. Recently World Heritage Committee solicited applications from World Heritage properties which had demonstrated new and creative ways of managing their sites. The Historic Town of Vigan in the Philippines was chosen as a best practice achieved with relatively limited resources, a good integration of the local community in many aspects of the sustainable conservation and management of the property and with an interesting multi-faceted approach to the protection of the site. Additionally, there are sites that include students from local schools in the management of the site (Slovenia), train local inhabitants as tour guides (Peru), or even put up nylon fences to protect villagers from straying tigers from the Sundarbans National Park (UNESCO, 2016c). In the management plan of sacred City of Caral-Supe several issues such as holistic approach, promotion of social development, involving and training of local people, master plan concerning sustainable development, interpretation of the site were recognized (UNESCO, 2016b).

One of the masterpieces of the Pala era, the Paharpur *Mahāvihāra* was the center of culture and administration of this region (Northern part of the Indian subcontinent) from at least seventh to tenth century CE. As if symbolic of the fate of archaeological edifices of this region, following the fall of the Pala dynasty, the *Mahāvihāra* virtually disappeared into oblivion for about seven centuries; having been entirely covered in earth. The site was first rediscovered by Buchanon Hamilton in the early decades of nineteenth century CE. Following Sir Alexander Cunningham's partial archaeological excavation in 1879, several excavations took place during the following three decades. Finally, in 1926 KN Dikshit unearthed the ground level of the *Mahāvihāra* (Alam, 2014). Recognizing the significance of this monument, Paharpur was declared as a 'World Heritage Site' in 1985 by the UNESCO (UNESCO, 2016a). Unfortunately, even after this recognition, over the last three decades there was no proper management plan and the site faced improper alterations, encroachment, theft, etc. These happened due to lack of proper maintenance, shortage of manpower, fund constraint, soil salinity, heavy rainfall, water logging and negligence. The severity of the damage can be understood from the loss of terracotta. Out of 2305

FIGURE 1.5: Panam Nagar
Panam Nagar was a township of rich Hindu merchants of British colonial era located at Sonargaon that flourished during the late 19th and early 20th century. The linear township consists of forty-nine abandoned street-front houses displaying hybrid form of British and local architectural style.

Source: Badruzzahan Ahmed

terracotta plaques found in 2004, a total of 595 completely eroded and at least 1810 rare terracotta figures in the storeroom of the site became a pile of ruins due to lack of preservation (Bilu, 2009).

Shatgumbad Mosque (Figure 1.3) at Khalifatabad (present day Bagerhat district of Khulna division), built by Khan al-Azam Ulugh Khan Jahan in the fifteenth century, is the largest of the Sultanate mosques in Bangladesh (Bari, 2014). The mosque displays an unique blend of indigenous elements with the imperial style of Delhi – at a time when the political and cultural life of independent Muslim Bengal clung obstinately to its provincial individuality (Ahmed & Alam, 1990). The magnificent monument turned into miserably decaying condition with the passage of time and similar to Paharpur *Mahāvihāra* the mosque was rediscovered and initially restored by the British colonial rulers. Recognizing the significance of this site,

FIGURE 1.6: Improper restoration at Panam Nagar
The Department of Archaeology undertook a conservation project and restored sixteen buildings at Panam Nagar. Due to lack of research, the department repeated mistakes similar to Paharpur, Shatgumbad and used unskilled workforce which led to damage of the original style.

Source: Author

Khalifatabad city including the Shatgumbad Mosque was declared as a 'World Heritage Site' in 1985 by the UNESCO (UNESCO, 2016a). Following this, there were several restoration attempts headed by the Department of Archaeology (responsible for preservation and protection of heritage sites) during the last three decades, resulting in distortion and damage of original architectural features. Among many improper alterations, one of the significant was when the original stone pillars of the Shatgumbad mosque was covered with ordinary cement plaster. This not only distorted the original feature of the mosque but narrowed the interior space. Under huge protest by the civil society this layer was recently removed.

Panam Nagar (Figure 1.5) was a township of rich Hindu merchants of British colonial era located at Sonargaon, former capital of Bengal during the Sultanate Period (Ahmed, 2006). The linear township flourished during the late nineteenth and early twentieth century. There are forty-nine abandoned street-front houses displaying hybrid form of British and local architectural style. Most of these houses were abandoned in the 1960s after local riots broke out following the partition of subcontinent in 1947, the rest left after the Liberation war of Bangladesh in 1971. From 1970s until 2004 the township was occupied by illegal inhabitants and became vulnerable with lack of maintenance or restoration. The Department of Archaeology listed

Panam Nagar as a protected archeological site in 2003 and vacated the township. Later, in 2006 the Department of Archaeology undertook a conservation project and restored sixteen buildings at various degree. Due to lack of research, the department repeated mistakes similar to Paharpur, Shatgumbad and used unskilled workforce which led to damage of the original style (Ali, 2007). The insensitive work (see Figure 1.6) was halted when the civil society and citizens protested and in 2008 Panam Nagar was listed as one of the 100 Most Endangered Sites by the World Monuments Fund (WMF, 2016).

To name a few, the historical documentation and heritage conservation attempts in this region discussed earlier shows a pattern of misinterpretation becoming popular belief and myths putting a veil over actual knowledge. The extent of this legacy has a cyclic effect on our perception of history, meaning of heritage, socioeconomic view of built spaces; often leading to large gaps in various areas of knowledge. Present trends in academia carries this pattern of misinterpretation that restricts the knowledge within the repetition of yet another cycle, rarely offering anything new. This raises the need to have a fresh outlook or rethink.

CONCEPT OF BENGAL

Symbolic places never represent a fixed and finalized historical fact but instead become the sites for the invention and reinvention of tradition while the past is reimagined (Azaryahu & Kellerman, 1999). Bengal (see Figure 1.1), the world's largest delta region, lies in the low-lying Ganges–Brahmaputra River Delta, commonly known as the Ganges Delta. Bengal is a great plain lying between the Himalayan Mountains and that part of the Indian Ocean known as the Bay of Bengal. It is dissected by a large number of rivers and the tributaries and distributaries of the Ganges or the Brahmaputra; its soil in most part being the alluvial deposition brought down by these rivers. The language generally spoken is Bengali and the country is known in that language as *Baṅgālāh* or *Baṅga-deś*, the country of *Baṅga*. The territory of Bengal extends over more than 94,000 square miles and is currently divided between two separate countries: the western part forms the state of West Bengal in India and the eastern part forms the country of Bangladesh.

Information on ancient Bengal is often contested, one of the reasons for this is the lack of appropriate evidence. The other is that only a small number of archaeological explorations have been conducted in this region due to shortage of funds, and almost all of these lasted only for a short period as investments dried up and bureaucratic barriers increased. In most cases, unfortunately therefore, one has to rely only on secondary and tertiary material to expose the ancient times. Hindu, Buddhist, Jain, Muslim literature, as well as, Greek, Roman, Chinese, Turkish, Afghan and Mughal documents are the familiar sources for the ancient history of this region (Thapar, 2004). In these evidences, Bengal is almost entirely absent. At the same time, there are hints strewn about in these texts regarding the region (Reza, 2012).

Though significant work has been done in archaeology, much of the material evidence of Bengal's glorious past has been washed away by the annual monsoon floods, the change of the course of rivers or more recently, through climatic alterations. Almost every ancient city in this region developed along one of its numerous rivers. Their change of course is so rapid and the effect so devastating that monsoon rains often wash away extensive stretches of their banks within a few days. On the other hand, due to the lack of availability of stone, local building materials such as wood and brick are more commonly used, but are not strong enough to withstand the onslaught of time and the climate.

Bearing footprint of many conquerors and rulers, this perhaps is the fate of Bengal; very similar to the alluvial soil of the Ganges Delta which gets a new layer of silt every year. This intricate layering can be observed in everywhere, including language, heritage, architecture and built environment. With the patina of age the layers get merged, transforms into something hybrid and in other cases information gets lost. To search for the origin and facts, it is essential to revisit and re-imagine.

CULTURE, SOCIAL LIFE AND HERITAGE

The rich geographic diversity of Bengal is probably expressed in Bengali culture which can be traced in everyday lifestyle of Bengali people, folklore, festivals, music, cinema, literature, cuisine, etc. Bengal has played important role in various philosophical and ideological movements such as Vajrayana (school of thought of Buddhism), *Vaishnava-Sahajiya* (form of tantric Vaishnavism), *Bauliana* (movement of mystic minstrels), abolition of *Swatidaho* (burning widows with their husbands), the *Swadeshi andolan* (freedom movement against the British), etc. These make the culture of Bengal unique and arguably considered amongst the richest in the Indian subcontinent.

Today's divided Bengal (West Bengal of India and Bangladesh) has emerged through a plethora of sociopolitical and religious events. However, the Bengali society and culture has a unique, singular origin when the local people (the Bang) settled in the region thousands of years ago. The Bengali culture has been enriched with imprints of many political empires, including the Gupta, Pala, Sen, Sultans of Buddhist, Hindu, Jain and Islamic origin, the Mughal and the British. Each has had a deep and profound impact over the culture. Reconfigured and reinterpreted through national level events and influences, each part has gradually formed its own niche of the overall Bengali culture. Often contextualized, this cultural division is only about seventy years old, i.e. post-partition of India and Pakistan in 1947. The core of society and culture that unites the Bengal region is thousands of years old, is deeply rooted in people's memory and soil. This 'undivided' culture, if one may call it so, has a much broader role to play in the society and culture of Bengal.

Like in an artist's canvas where many incoherent pieces often mix and match to make a whole, cultural layers often blends with each other where it becomes difficult to trace back to a singular source. Many elements of Bengali culture are the inheritance of Hindu, Buddhist, Islamic and other regional influences. While some had their inspirations from these sources, others are the true fruit of local soil carried through tangible and intangible heritage elements that are unique to this region. Probably the land has this distinctive character that it could adapt foreign elements to the level that they become Bengal's own. Starting with the Aryans, most of the invaders had chosen not to conquer Bengal; rather they became settlers and in time they evolved as Bengali and their culture became part of local culture. This dichotomy between foreign stylistic imports and internal indigenous elements has created myriad cultural elements that stand out as Bengal's own such as *Jamdani, Nakshi Katha, Jatra, Putul Nach, Puja, Boishakhi, Baul, Jari, Shari, Bhawaiya, Bhatiali, Gambhira, Charyapada, Padabali, Mangol kabbo, Puthi, Shukta, Pot chitra*, terracotta, etc.

Despite a border of two countries dividing the region, the society and culture of Bengal has a united soul (what it means to be a *Bangali*) though the details may vary in places. One feels its presence in all the elements mentioned above; even though there are local interpretations. There are areas to be explored where this local or regional features (often with external inspirations) had impact on architecture, heritage and built environment.

EPILOGUE

It should be noted that the vast area of knowledge mentioned above cannot be addressed in a single compilation. However, the studies attempted here give a glimpse of a few selected areas of knowledge. *Matsayana*, the obscure part of pre-Pala phase has been re-investigated here challenging the customary approach to assign any medieval Buddhist architectural contributions to the Pala kings. Challenging the urban decay of post-Gupta India, this study shows the possible existence of urban settlements in Bengal through the presence of socioeconomic development and architecture during that period. In study of Pundranagar, hierarchies of the traditional spatial pattern of a medieval walled city of Gaur is analyzed. In case of Panam Nagar, all the existing studies strongly focus on its heritage value and subsequently lacks any attempts to uncover the possibilities of these hybrid houses in terms of adapted architectural spaces. An attempt to explore this uncharted territory, addressing the issue at urban and architectural scale is presented.

Heritage management in this region is generally bureaucratic where the community attachment to local heritage is rarely considered, resulting in *soulless* restorations, gentrification, etc. Two studies present alternate approaches in the context of traditional urban settlements and archaeological sites. The shaded area of community involvement in heritage management with its local mechanism has been rarely explored for traditional enclaves of Bengal. The first attempt shows the influence of social capital over community based informal heritage management in Old Dhaka. The second study attempts to identify the risks and threats that archaeological sites face in Bangladesh, review the compatibility of the existing conservation legislations and finally recommend a strategic management plan suggesting possible local community involvement.

It is only natural that this book makes a small attempt to unveil the large diaspora of knowledge that the region offers. By no means comprehensive, it still brings new ideas and questions in front which no doubt will spark further investigation. When it does, and inevitably it will as there is a necessity. Perhaps this will be the contribution of this effort in its small way.

REFERENCES

- Ahmed, I. (2006). A Participatory Approach to Conservation: Working with Community to Save the Cultural Heritage of Panamnagar. *BRAC University Journal*, III(2), 25-33.
- Ahmed, I. (2012). *A study of architectural heritage management by the informal community bodies in traditional neighborhoods of old Dhaka.* (Doctor of Philosophy), National University of Singapore, Singapore.
- Ahmed, N., & Alam, A. K. M. S. (1990). Architectural Conservation Of Paharpur And Bagerhat. In A. H. Imamuddin & K. R. Longeteig (Eds.), *Architectural and Urban Conservation in the Islamic World* (pp. 110-120). Geneva: The Aga Khan Trust for Culture.
- Ahmed, N., Ali, M., Alam, M. S., & Musa, M. A. (2000). *History of Dhaka Through Inscription and Architecture A Portrait of the Sultanate.* Dhaka: Ministry of Cultural Affairs, Government of the People's Republic of Bangladesh.
- Alam, M. S. (2014). Paharpur. In S. Islam & A. J. Ahmed (Eds.), *Banglapedia* (2 ed.). Dhaka: Asiatic Society of Bangladesh.
- Ali, T. (2007, 26 April). Panamnagar: Unscientific restoration defacing heritage. *The Daily Star*. Retrieved from http://archive.thedailystar.net/2007/04/26/d7042601107.htm
- Azaryahu, M., & Kellerman, A. (1999). Symbolic places of national history and revival: a study in Zionist mythical geography. *Transactions of the Institute of British Geographers, 24*(1), 109–123. doi: 10.1111/j.0020-2754.1999.00109.x
- Banu, R. A. (1992). *Islam in Bangladesh* (Vol. 58): Brill.
- Bari, M. (2014). Shatgumbad Mosque. In S. Islam & A. J. Ahmed (Eds.), *Banglapedia* (2 ed.). Dhaka: Asiatic Society of Bangladesh.
- Begum, A. (2014). Bakht Binat's Mosque. In S. Islam & A. J. Ahmed (Eds.), *Banglapedia* (2 ed.). Dhaka: Asiatic Society of Bangladesh.
- Bilu, H. R. (2009, April 25). World heritage site left in ruins: Terracotta artefacts at Paharpur monastery damaged due to lack of maintenance. *The Daily Star*.
- Eaton, R. M. (1993). *The Rise of Islam and the Bengal Frontier, 1204-1760.* Berkeley: University of California Press.
- Eaton, R. M. (2004). *Temple Desecration and Muslim States in Medieval India.* New Delhi: Hope India Publications.
- Fischer, D. H. (1970). *Historians' Fallacies: Toward a logic of historical thought.* New York: Harper Perennial.
- Haque, E. (2009). *Dhaka alias Jahangirnagar: 400 Years.* Dhaka: the International Centre for Study of Bengal Art.
- ICAHM. (1990). *Charter for the protection and management of the archaeological heritage.* Paper presented at the The 9th General Assembly of ICOMOS, Lausanne, Switzerland.

- ICOMOS. (1964, May 25-31). *The Venice Charter (International charter for the conservation and restoration of monuments and sites)*. Paper presented at the The Second International Congress of Architects and Technicians of Historical Monuments, Venice.
- Munslow, A. (2006). *Deconstructing History*: Taylor & Francis.
- Powell, R., Lim, A. K. S., & Invernizzi, L. (1994). *Living legacy: Singapore's architectural heritage renewed*: Singapore Heritage Society.
- Reza, M. H. (2008). Bengal Gupta Viharas_Did such a Phenomenon Exist. *The International Journal of Interdisciplinary Social Science, 3*(5), 211-216.
- Reza, M. H. (2010). Post Gupta Bengal- Inscriptions, Coins and Literatures. *Journal of Eurasian Studies, 2*(4), 22-28.
- Reza, M. H. (2012). *Early Buddhist Architecture of Bengal: Morphological study on the vihāras of c. 3rd to 8th centuries.* (Doctor of Philosophy), Nottingham Trent University, Nottingham.
- Reza, M. H., Bandyopadhyay, S., & Mowla, A. (2015). Traces of Buddhist Architecture in Gupta and post-Gupta Bengal: Evidence from Inscriptions and Literature. *Journal of Eurasian Studies*, VII(3), 9-19.
- Salomon, R. (1998). *Indian Epigraphy: A Guide to the Study of Inscriptions in Sanskrit Prakrit and Other Indo-Aryan Languages*. Oxford: Oxford University Press.
- Sarkar, J. N. (1972). *Islam in Bengal : thirteenth to nineteenth century* (Fifth ed.). Calcutta: Ratna Prakashan.
- Shahnewaz, A., & Haque, M. M. (2014, November 10, 2014). Charsho noy Hajar bochor. *Daily ittefaq*.
- Thapar, R. (2010). *Syndicated Hinduism*: Critical Quest.
- UNESCO. (2003, 17 October). *Convention for the Safeguarding of the Intangible Heritage*, Paris.
- UNESCO. (2016a). Inscription: Ruins of the Buddhist Vihara at Paharpur (Bangladesh).   Retrieved 1 June, 2016, from http://whc.unesco.org/en/decisions/3838
- UNESCO. (2016b). Sacred City of Caral-Supe.   Retrieved 18 May, 2016, from http://whc.unesco.org/en/list/1269/bestpractice
- UNESCO. (2016c). Sharing best practices in World Heritage management.   Retrieved 18 May, 2016, from http://whc.unesco.org/en/recognition-of-best-practices/
- UNESCO. (2016d). Traditional Ainu dance.   Retrieved 16 May, 2016, from http://www.unesco.org/culture/ich/en/RL/traditional-ainu-dance-00278
- UNESCO, ICCROM, & ICOMOS. (1994, 1-6 November). *The Nara Document on Authenticity*. Paper presented at the Nara Conference on Authenticity in Relation to the World Heritage Convention, Nara, Japan.
- WMF. (2016). 2016 World Monuments Watch.   Retrieved 8 June, 2016, from https://www.wmf.org/watch/watch_year/2008

FIGURE 2.1: Conjectural reconstruction of the early cruciform shrine of post-Gupta Bengal
The absence of archaeological evidence makes it difficult to perceive the superstructure of any post-Gupta shrine. This conjectural reconstruction is based on the morphological analysis of architectural forms.

Source: Author

RETHINKING THE POST-GUPTA BENGAL: SETTLEMENT AND ARCHITECTURE

Mohammad Habib Reza

Arguably, the post-Gupta period is considered a grey phase in the history of Bengal. Lack of enough historical evidence makes it so, and a group of historians stands behind to support it which established it as a relatively dark period. Especially since 1897 CE, when the Kalimpur copper plate inscription of Dharmapala was found, the period before the Pala dynasty was marked as the *Maṭsaṇṇaya*, a state of political chaos and anarchy (Pal, 2008; Griffiths, 2015). Many historians found it in tune with their philosophy and accepted it without a great debate. In fact, there were enough evidence to mark this period contested with a great political chaos. Available resources suggest that the decline of the Gupta kingdom in the sixth century CE led to the growth of many small kingdoms in certain regions. It is that time when many Gupta vassals freed themselves from the sovereignty of the Gupta's by founding independent kingdoms (Willis, 2005; Kumar, 2005-6). In addition, there are enough evidences showing these kingdoms were at war among themselves to establish their authority. Finally, powerful political dynasties like the Mukharis, the Hunas and the later Magadhan Guptas had successfully captured some parts and became rulers of Bengal.

The colonial and nationalist scholars had much to say about this dark period; arguably they wanted to project Bengal as a single political and cultural entity from the Pala period onward. The Gupta Empire was considered as the classical period, in art and architecture (Figure 2.2), for the northern India (Smith, 1914); whereas, the Pala period, commencing from the accession of its first ruler Gopala in the late eighth century CE, was considered as 'golden age' in the history of Bengal (Majumdar, 1943). Both the Gupta and Pala were the ruler of the greater part of north India and played a significant role in shaping what was portrayed as the key character of unified India. To glorify

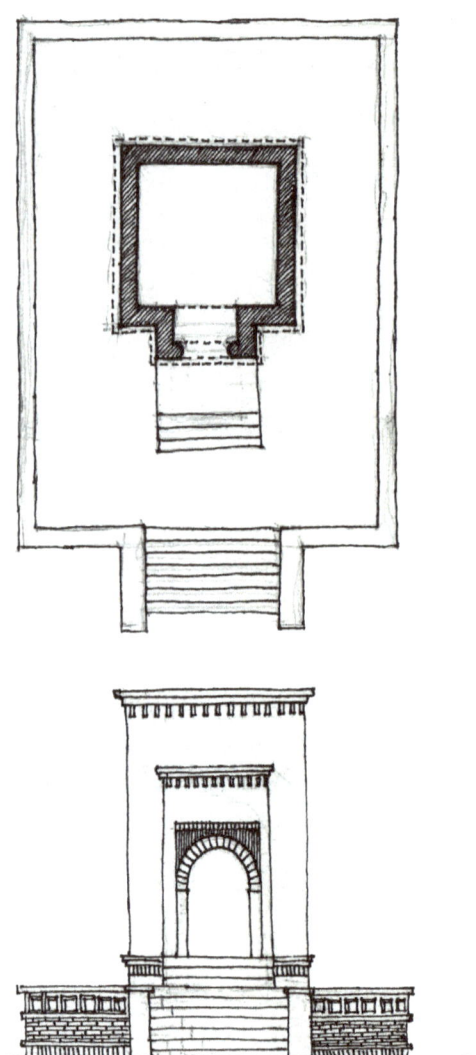

FIGURE 2.2: Early Gupta shrine
A typical Gupta shrine, considered the classical form of North Indian shrine. The post-Gupta shrines have evolved from this classical form.

Source: Author

these larger empires, periods in between have never been formally recognized. Rather, they were kept under shade to glorify the larger empires even more. The concept of this 'dark period' is not a new phenomenon in the global context, there are many similar attempts that could facilitate understanding this 'dark period' syndrome. Most popular among them is the European dark age before the Renaissance; this period was simply ignored to glorify the Christian supremacy and to keep achievements of the Islamic empire under

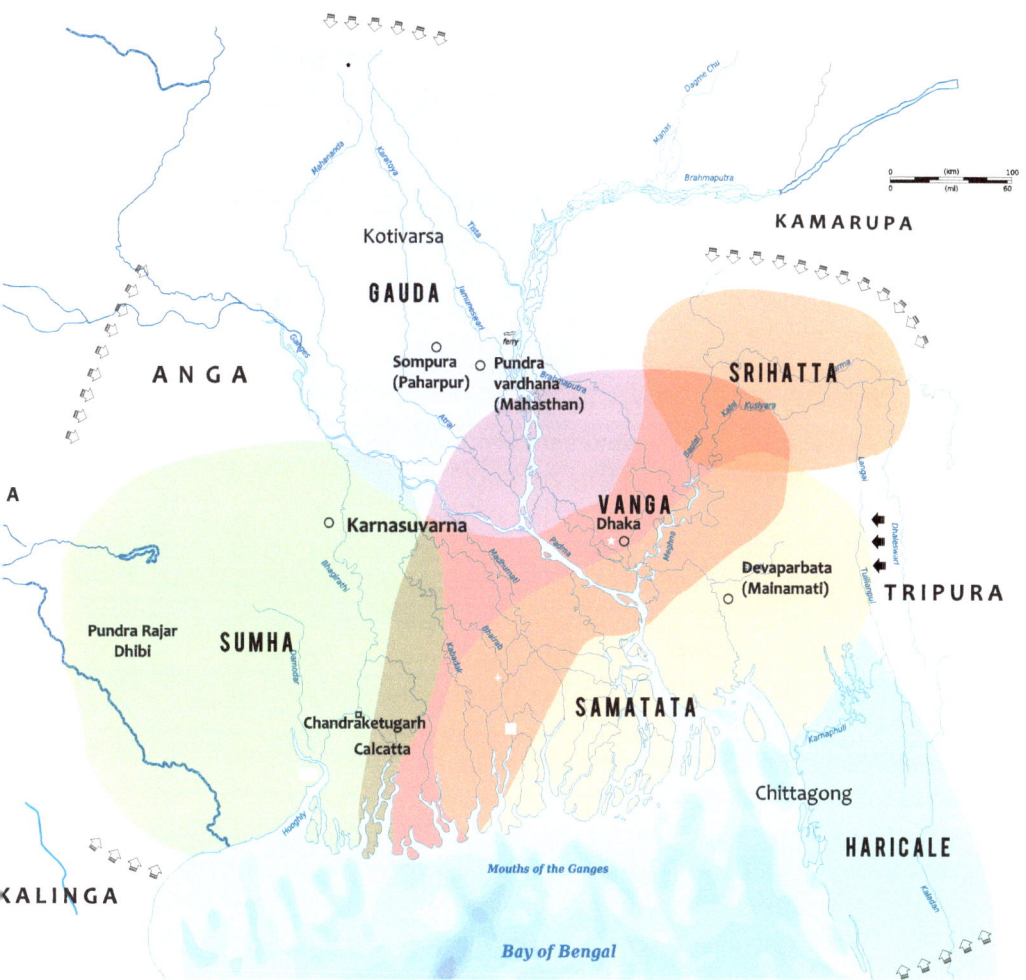

FIGURE 2.3: Bengal during the post-Gupta period
Rise of the Gauda and the Vaṇga or Samataṭa kingdoms.

Source: Author

cover. In the history of Islam this dark period was marked as the golden age. In global context this period was a cultural peak that saw many scientific, cultural and literary innovations and ideas that enriched the later periods. There is a precedence of 'dark period' in the Islamic world too; long before the European dark age, Islam declares the periods just before its evolution as the darkest time and not worthy of exploring (mentioned in Islamic literature as *Ayame Zaheliyat* or 'age of the ignorant' in Arabic). Many Islamic scholars believed it and continued to establish it through their works. In case of the post-Gupta period, the colonial and nationalist scholars had enough reasons to believe this and establish it. Whereas the later scholars, some of those who grew up with this idea, blindly followed their predecessors' path.

Fortunately, identification of new historical resources inspired many scholars to feel the veracity of *Matsannaya* and challenge the existing ideas. With the independence of India, nationalist sentiment emerged as the reaction to the then scholars of the colonial movement. This facilitated path to rethinking of many established ideas as the colonial philosophies gradually faded away. The shaded post-Gupta period was eventually questioned and light has been shed recognizing the political and social aspects of that era. The pioneer scholars rethinking this part of history could be marked as the contemporary historians. Whereas, the scholars who grew up with the colonial or nationalist sentiment and followed it blindly are still in the dark. Unfortunately, many archaeologists working in this region are not yet open to the contemporary ideas and their works are continuously deteriorating the scope of rethinking, making the historical perspective more complex. Preconceived ideas force them to 'worship' some historical issues which is in tune with their thoughts and ignore others who are not. Eventually this attitude has significant impact on the architectural history of Bengal as archaeological data is the primary source for the study of any historical architecture. It is especially relevant to study of any medieval architecture that highly depends on archaeological findings and analysis. Therefore, it is obvious that study of settlements and architecture of the post-Gupta Bengal faces the same challenge and needs rethinking.

The challenges to identify the charterers of the post-Gupta Bengal's settlements and architecture are many. The previously stated twisted theory subsequently developed many misunderstanding and myths about the period. As architecture or settlement pattern is closely connected with its socioeconomic background, a proper contextual study could help to understand the settlement and architecture of this period. To have a wider understanding of the social and economic conditions of the post-Gupta period, established myths should be rethought and re-examined with the light of recent archaeological findings and unbiased analysis. Some popular theories in the field of architectural history of the post-Gupta Bengal that need to be re-examined at this point for an unbiased understanding of this period are as follows:

- There were many small kingdoms in Bengal during the post-Gupta period who were fighting between themselves. The rulers of these small kingdoms didn't have enough time to contribute in architecture.
- Lack of strong rulers (great kings) suggests lesser economic

power, which is very insignificant in comparison with that of the great Gupta period. There was a limited possibility to contribute in architecture by these lesser rulers with their weak economic condition.
- India, specifically the northern part, had urban decline during the post-Gupta period. So there is a high probability that Bengal had an urban decay during this period.
- The scant archaeological findings before Pala period suggests the absence of any significant architecture of the post-Gupta period.

There is no doubt that the decline of the Gupta kingdom gave rise to many small kingdoms in Bengal as Gupta vassals freed themselves from the sovereignty by founding independent kingdoms (Figure 2.3). Probably, as an offshoot of the Imperial Gupta, the later Gupta continued the tradition of Gupta sovereignty in the central and Eastern part of the Gupta empire from Magadha and Malwa (Reza, 2010). Prominent twentieth century historian Majumdar rightfully points out that taking the advantages of the political situation two powerful kingdoms evolved in Bengal during this period: the Gauda and the *Vaṇga* or *Samataṭa* kingdoms emerged through merging of many small kingdoms (Majumdar, 1943). The Gauda was primary mainly target for the outsiders like the Mukharis, the Hunas and the Harshavardhana to capture and control as it was located adjacent to Magadha. The later Gupta rulers also had certain control over the Gauda kingdom till 650 CE. On the contrary, by the virtue of its location the *Vaṇga* or *Samataṭa* was far away from the reach of many powerful regional kings of India. Though it was not unconquerable, no significant capture could be identified where any outsider had control over this region for a long time. This perhaps helped to develop local dynasties such as the Khadga (c. 625 CE - 725 CE), the Rata (c. 650 CE - 675 CE) and the early Deva[1] (c. 750 CE - 850 CE); who ruled this part of Bengal for generations (Reza, Bandyopadhyay et al. 2015).

It is yet to be identified, how long it took to build the significant early medieval architecture of Bengal. Historical resources provide enough clues with certainty that essential phases of construction of the late medieval marvel, the Taj Mahal, was completed in at least 11 years (1631 - 1642 CE); it took another decade to complete the other phases (Carroll and Newsweek, 1973). Similarly, another significant Mughal monument, the Humayun's tomb, took about eight years to be built (1565 - 1572 CE) (Blanshard & Blanshard, 1992). There are further resources, suggesting many monuments in this region were continued to be built through generations. It can be easily assumed that the significant early medieval complexes such as Sompura *mahāvihāra* took years to be built; it could have been even more than decades as the building technology was more primal than the Mughals. However, other smaller constructions should not have taken that much time. The monastic tradition of the early medieval period further suggests there is a possibility of voluntary monastic community participation in the construction process. Inclusion of these self-motivated and dedicated personals of the religious communities could remarkably reduce the construction time of any building. Keeping these issues in mind, it can be assumed with some certainty that many post-Gupta kings had enough time to build similar small buildings in their kingdoms if their economy supported. Comparatively powerful dynasties such as the Khadga, the Rata and the early Deva even had enough scope to build much larger building complexes.

The *Gauda* and the *Vaṇga* were enjoying independence to some extent during the post-Gupta period. Though imperial power by its definition suggests the ability of large economic strength, an independent smaller kingdom had scope to achieve significant economic strength too, as they did not have to pay tax to the central government. Along with this, few powerful kings managed to expand their territory to the adjacent kingdoms of Bengal. Ultimately, the *Vaṇga* kingdom extended its boundary to almost all southern and southwestern parts of Bengal during some powerful kings.

Urbanization in the early mediaeval India had been a matter of debate among many historians. The popular stream are the followers of the twentieth century historian Sharma, who had argued in his most popular work *Urban Decay in India*. In this book he proposes that there were a two-stage de-urbanisation in the early mediaeval India: the first one was after the third century CE and the second one was after the sixth century CE (Sharma, 1987). To establish this, he presented a brief and systematic overview of 132 early historic sites across India. It is evident that his attempt was to establish a single economic state for the early mediaeval north India. Whereas, looking for a single economic state for the post-Gupta period does not sound rational at all due to the presence of complex economic condition during this period. Through a particular area based study Kennet argued that the archaeological evidence for urban decay was far from 'unassailable' and the chronology of events was a 'matter of speculation' (Kennet, 2013). He further stated that the urban decay never happened at all and the whole theory was based on the poor archaeological methodology. Adopting a stand contrary to Sharma, Chattopadhyaya in his *The Making of Early Medieval India* argues that the early medieval period saw the decline of some urban centres, while others simultaneously continued to flourish and some new ones also emerged (Chattopadhyaya, 1996). This argument fits better with Bengal; archaeological findings further confirm that there was decline of previous flourishing cities such as *Tamraliptiī, Baṇgaṛh* were declining; *Puṇḍravardhaṇa, Karṇasuvarṇa* and many more cities were continued to flourish; and *Samataṭa, Kotalipara* and so on emerged. In addition, from the economic point of view, Chakravarti, in his *Trade and Traders in Early Indian Society* strongly argues against the perception of declining trade in India during 600–1000 CE and demonstrates the linkages of trade at the locality level during this period (Chakravarti, 2002).

In fact, the post-Gupta period was a transitional period between two significant North Indian empires, as well as a bridge between these two cultures. The religious beliefs of the Gupta rulers were predominantly Vaishnavism whereas the Pala were *Vajrayāna* (Tantric *Mahayana*) believers. The religious fabric of the post-Gupta Bengal was also in the transitional phase between the Vaishnavism and the *Vajrayāna* Buddhism. The actual sceneries were more complex to express by a simple statement due to the individuality of these kingdoms. Again, the religious inclination of any ruler does not confirm that the people of that religion were majority of that kingdom. Explored archaeological findings until now could only provide enough evidences to confirm the religious inclination of the rulers, whereas ample evidences are missing to give a comprehensive view of the then people's religion. Historical evidences confirm that the religious inclination of a ruler simply provided privilege to the group of people who followed the same religion. These evidences further suggest that many rulers were open enough to contribute towards other religions too. That actually suggests presence of diversity in the religious fabric and strong position of the other believers in the society.

According to the Jain tradition, Bengal was one of the four places where Jainism spread at the earlier stage of the religion (c. sixth century BCE). There is enough reason to believe that the Digambara, one of the two major schools of Jainism, were a major group of people in Bengal in the ancient period. It is yet to be examined why their number reduced with time and at what point they almost vanished from this region, it is safe to state that a huge number of *Digambara* were present in Bengal during the Gupta and post-Gupta period. Whereas, Buddhist tradition suggests Buddha (c. 563 BCE - 483 BCE) himself had visited some part of *Puṇḍravardhaṇa* during his lifetime (Chakma, 2008). Especially the discovery of a Maurya inscription, coins and other artifacts at the Mahasthan bear testimony that Buddhism had established a powerful footing in Bengal during Asoka's reign (reign c. 268 to 232 BCE). Literary sources also support that Asoka had built stupas at *Tamraliptiī, Karṇasuvarṇa, Puṇḍravardhaṇa* and *Samataṭa* in Bengal. From Buddha to Asoka, Buddhism became so deeply rooted in the heart of the people that probably other rulers could not wipe it out from Bengal. That is why, Hieun Tsang found Buddhist people as the majority and the *Digambara* as second in *Puṇḍravardhaṇa* in the post-Gupta period during his visit (Beal, 1885).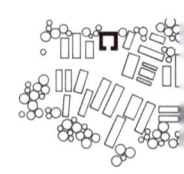

The Gupta age settlements predominantly had single or multiple temples to perform their religious activities, there are enough ethnographic research record that supports rulers' contribution towards these temples. With a sharp contrast, most recorded Pala settlements are predominantly monastic and there are many records of rulers' contribution towards these monastic settlements. Available archaeological resources further suggest these monastic settlements were a concentration of huge population; some of them were accommodating more than thousand monks. There was also a concentration of the few monasteries as a neighbor, which in return suggests available settlement concentration within a close proximity. There is a historical tradition of fort city or port city due to settlements evolving around these to support their services. Most probably, these monasteries had settlements around them, which suggest an urban fabric similar to but earlier versions of the present day university cities. The religious practices of that period further suggest settlements in proximity to perform the daily activities of the monks (see Figure 2.4).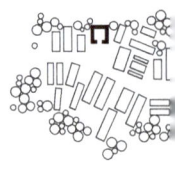

The common trend in Bengal was that the rulers used to build their administrative centres considering the potential of the area; famous religious localities and forthcoming commerce and trading-oriented areas used to attract them (Doza, 2016). The third category is the fort city, which was exclusively developed around a fort. There are many examples of erection of forts at a place, which was not highly populated, but was significant in terms of defense from the invading kingdoms. Most probably the fortress cities such as, *Mahasthangarh*,

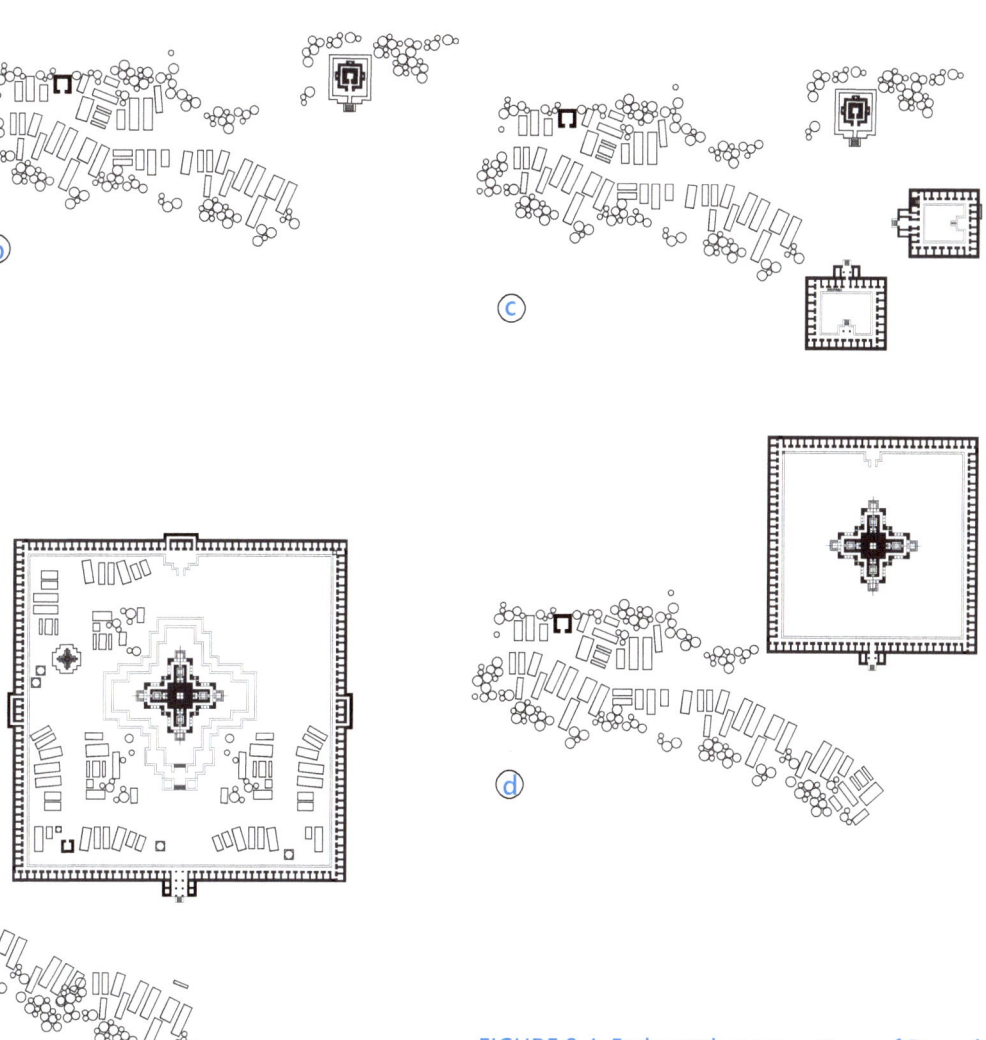

FIGURE 2.4: Early settlement pattern of Bengal
The figure shows evolution of religious settlements from the early Gupta to later Pala period. The Gupta age settlements had predominantly single or multiple temples; through a series of complex development phases it reached the advanced form of later Pala period.

Source: Author

Nandangarh, Pataliputra, Kotivarsha, Rampal, Ramabati, Karṇasuvarṇa etc. had similar reasons to evolve. Until the Gupta period, most flourishing cities were located in these areas where the commerce and trading potentiality was high. Probably this was happening due to the economic orientation of imperial power and their detachment from the local religious alignment. The other reason is that the Vaishnavism did not promote monasticism as the Buddhist practice

FIGURE 2.5: Early post-Gupta shrine
Shrines of the post-Gupta period had gone through multiplication, enlargement, consolidation or recombination of elements found in the shrines of their predecessor.

Source: Author

did which in turn generated concentration of human settlements. As many small kingdoms evolved align with the local religious inclination, many rulers of that period were Buddhist; the post-Gupta period of Bengal have seen many cities evolving around a religious nucleus. Considering this context, it can be assumed that the transition of the post-Gupta settlement from the Gupta settlement could have followed the stages shown in Figure 2.4.

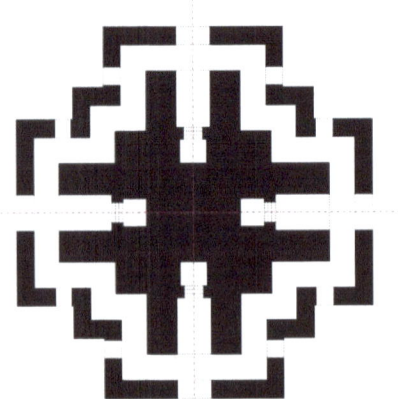

FIGURE 2.6: Cruciform shrine of Bengal
Bengal's unique contribution towards the evolution of cruciform Buddhist shrine. The development pattern suggests that this phase was developed in the Vaṇga or Samataṭa kingdoms plan of the earlier version of cruciform shrine explored at the Rupbanmura vihāra, Comilla

Source: Author

FIGURE 2.7: Incorporation of crown to the shrine
Development of the superstructure from Gupta flat roof to post-Gupta Śikhara.

Source: Author

In case of architecture, there are strong evidences to believe that only the significant structures were made of brick (with some stone elements) to make them permanent, others were temporary structures of perishable materials such as wood or mud. These temporary wooden or earthen structures naturally decayed in the harsh climate of Bengal. On the other hand, permanent structures were able to survive longer withstanding the harsh condition. Despite this, the fact remains that the brick structures had a lesser chance of surviving so long compared to the stone structures of other places where stone was available. Little is known about the superstructures of these brick structures and only remains of the substructures has been identified. Till now most of the explored archaeological remains of the medieval structures of Bengal are of permanent type, which are primarily the remains of forts, fortification walls, shrines and monasteries. One of the significant settlement patterns of the post-Gupta Bengal was settlements evolving around a religious nucleus; religious structures were significant and evolved to satisfy the socio-religious requirements and eventually bears the testimony of that time.

Shrine as a Vedic religious space may have long existed since the early historic period. Whereas evolution of *Garbhagriha* is fairly new, authentic traces have not gone back before the beginning of the Common Era. *Garbhagriha* is the innermost sanctum to reside the primary deity, literally means womb chamber from Sanskrit words

FIGURE 2.8: Development of cruciform shrine
Significant development phases of Bengali Buddhist shrine, from rectangular to cruciform plan.

Source: Author

garbha meaning womb and *griha* meaning house. Generally, the *Garbhagriha* is a square space with an entry, which might have taken the shape before the Gupta period. The Guptas were the first to build the purpose-built shrines which evolved from the earlier tradition of rock-cut shrines influenced by Kusana, Mathura and Gandhara styles. Most temples adopt a square plan with the single cubicle Garbhagriha in the center, normally entered by a highly decorated doorway with a projecting lintel. The Gupta identification mark is the addition of the short columned porch at the entrance. In the earlier phase of the Gupta period, the shrine was flat roofed (Figure 2.2). Discovered terracotta plaques from many archaeological sites suggest the

presence of the flat roofed Gupta shrine in Bengal (Haque, 2007). The advance Gupta shrines further added a rectangular platform with a single flight of steps in front aligned with the entrance (see Figure 2.6, 2.7 & 2.8).

The post-Gupta style architecture is often patently experimental (Harle, 1977), to cope with the transitional nature of socio-religious movements which was going through many changes. Shrines of this period has gone through multiplication, enlargement, consolidation or recombination of elements found in the shrines of their predecessor. In addition, new elements were introduced to satisfy the changing socio-religious requirements which the existing models had limited scope to answer. This transitional state consequently led towards many innovative solutions and finally generated the unique blend of the Śikhara-śirsha-bhadra superstructure with the cruciform plan (Reza, 2013). Before reaching this ultimate point, the builders had gone through the trial and error process, which can be traced in many excavated archaeological sites of Bengal. There are two significant visible developments: firstly, on the plan; and the other in the superstructure (see Figure 2.8).

This short discussion regarding the post-Gupta settlements and architecture of Bengal through historical analysis is certainly inadequate to provide a comprehensive picture. However, it leaves little doubt that there were numerous settlements and architecture in Bengal during the centuries spanning the post-Gupta rulers of Bengal, both important and less significant ones. It is important to note that, contrary to generally held views, significant contributions towards settlements and architecture by the post-Gupta regional and local rulers shows a remarkable and continued presence of distinct style in Bengal.

This chapter is an attempt to understand the socio-cultural fabric of the post-Gupta Bengal through their settlements and architecture. The scarcity of archaeological findings has definitely limited the scope to have a clear perspective of that time. However, it shows how far an unbiased attempt could take us. This understanding could be challenged or further refined to accommodate new findings; it only aims that fellow researchers will come up with new ideas to challenge or refine this theory with their researches. If so, these brainstorming will impact not only the twisted understanding of the post-Gupta period, but also the whole ancient and medieval history of Bengal. In the history of Bengal architecture, this is an attempt to push the start point of the bracket of mediaeval time of Bengal about two centuries backwards, which eventually push back the end point of the ancient time bracket.

ENDNOTE

1 The Early Deva or Hindu Deva dynasty (which is not to be confused with the Buddhist Deva dynasty of the thirteenth century) may have been the last important native dynasty in Bengal. They were contemporary to the great Pala Empire and were able to rule the *Vaṅga* kingdom from c. 750 CE to c. 850 CE.

REFERENCE

- Beal, S. (1885). *Buddhist records of the western world.*
- Carroll, D. and i. B. D. Newsweek (1973). The Taj Mahal, *Newsweek*.
- Catherine Blanshard, A. and A. Catherine Ella Blanshard (1992). *Architecture of Mughal India*, Cambridge University Press.
- Chakma, N. K. (2008). Buddhism. *Banglapedia*. P. S. Islam. Dhaka, Asiatic Society of Bangladesh.
- Chakravarti, R. (2002). *Trade and Traders in Early Indian Society*, Manohar.
- Chattopadhyaya, B. (1996). *The Making of Early Medieval India*, Oxford University Press.
- Doza, S. B. (2016). *Riverine fortress city of `Mahasthan´ in deltaic Bengal: In search for the traditional settlement pattern of ancient cities.* Doctor of Philosophy, University of Évora.
- Griffiths, A. (2015). "New Documents for the Early History of Pupdravardhana: Copperplate Inscriptions from the Late Gupta and Early Post-Gupta Periods." *Pratna Samiksha* 6: 15-38.
- Haque, E. (2007). *The Art Heritage of Bangladesh*, International Centre for Study of Bengal Art.
- Harle, J. C. (1977). "The post_Gupta style in Indian temple architectue and sculpture." *Journal of the Royal Society of Arts* 125(5253): 570-589.
- Kennet, D. (2013). *Reconsidering the decline of urbanism in late Early Historic and Early Medieval South Asia.* Les préludes de l'Islam. C. J. Robin and J. Schiettecatte. Paris, France, De Boccard: 331-353.
- Kumar, A. (2005-6). *Changing faces of Gupta and post Gupta towns of Bengal.* Indian History Congress, Santiniketan, Kolkata.
- Majumdar, R. C. (1943). *The History of Bengal.* Dhaka, The University of Dacca.
- Pal, S. (2008). "Matsyanyaya of Khalimpur Inscription : Revisiting its Geo-Historical Significance." *Journal of the Asiatic Society* L(2): 21-36.
- Reza, M. H. (2010). "Post Gupta Bengal - Inscriptions, Coins and Literatures." *Journal of Eurasian Studies* 2(4): 22-28.
- Reza, M. H. (2013). *Early Buddhist Architecture of Bengal: Morphological study on the vihāras of c. 3rd to 8th centuries.* Doctor of Philosophy, Nottingham Trent University.
- Reza, M. H., S. Bandyopadhyay and A. Mowla (2015). "Traces of Buddhist Architecture in Gupta and post-Gupta Bengal: Evidence from Inscriptions and Literature." *Journal of Eurasian Studies* VII(3): 9-19.
- Sharma, R. S. (1987). *Urban decay in India, c. 300-c. 1000*, Munshiram Manoharlal Publishers.
- Smith, V. A. (1914). *Indian Sculpture of the Gupta Period A.D. 300-650*, Oesterheld & Company.
- Willis, M. (2005). "Later Gupta History: Inscriptions, Coins and Historical Ideology." *Journal of the Royal Asiatic Society (Third Series)* 15(2): 131-150.

FIGURE 3.1: Gumti gate
Brilliant works of enamel tiles work on the terracotta bricks structure of Gumti gate (1512 CE).

Source: Author

PUNDRANAGAR: THE OTHER STORY OF A MEDIEVAL WALLED CITY OF GAUR

Sajid Bin Doza

INTRODUCTION

The victory of the empire was written in the manuscript; these scripts tell the royal-vigorous lifestyle and the reign of paramount rulers, used to be written by the King's attendant to document their part of the history. The political, socio-cultural and economic phenomena found their place in the narratives, similar to empires in other parts of the world. It is rather common that history and literature talks about the mighty king with fabulous art and architecture and their contribution to the society.

South Asia was no different; historical narratives took place only for the great emperor and the kingdom; during Asoka's time, the art and architecture was detailed only for the sake of the 'imperial interest'. The great Asoka triumphal columns and the stupa of Sanchi (c. third century BCE) at Bhopal were dedicated to Buddhism and the pilgrims. Even in the Hinayana and Mahayana phases the art and architecture was dominated by religious notion (Tadgell, 2002). The Ajanata and the Elora caves, masterpieces of architecture and precious milestones in the rock cut form, were built with the inherent intention of placing schools of religious studies in a very remote and introverted place.

The Gupta period in the subcontinent became famous for the plastic arts, subsequently the stone crafting spread all over the subcontinent. The famous Durga temple at Aihole and the Ladkhan temple was erected with strong concepts during the reign of Chaluccan order (c. 450 CE). But who built these all? Who are the people behind the making of brilliant craftsmanship? We have a very obscure conception about them as history provides very little detail. These laborious people who built these masterpieces of that period, but had never been nourished in the pages of historical literature. This is an attempt

FIGURE 3.2: Bengal and Assam in the ninteenth century
Bengal region during the British period showing political boundaries.

Source: British Library Images online

to identify and analyze the common story of the traditional areas; of the people that lived by the fortified walls.

During the Pala period, the revival of stone crafting reached the highest pick; Pala sculptures took the position of sophisticated emblem of creating sculpture in black basalt stone. Palas created a massive structure at the time, known as the Sompur Vihara (seventh century CE) (Ahmed, 1984), which is considered the largest intelligent brick architecture in the subcontinent. The magnificent structure was built to show the dynasty's ability and the entity. Bengal flourished as the land of Buddhism during the time, but the social structure of the period is never shown in the historical documentation.

Due to scarce evidence, little is known of the cultural legitimacy of the region during the sultanate period. However, the history of the period shows proper annotation about the fort arena and the religious architecture. During the sultanate period, six influential

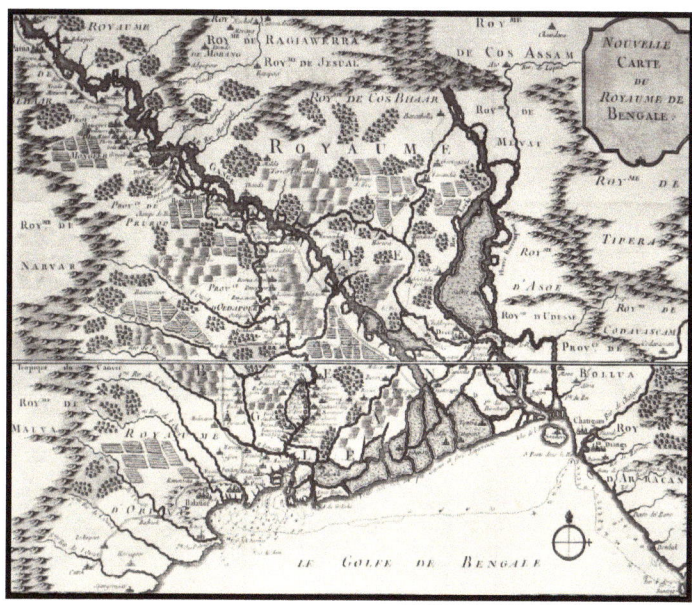

FIGURE 3.3: Bengal in the seventeenth century
Map of Bengal by the Portuguese.

Source: Banglapedia

styles[1] generated in Bengal. Among them the Ilyas Shahi (1435-1487 CE) and the Hussain Shahi (1494-1538 CE) (Dani, 1961; Ahmed, 1980; Hasan, 2007) period is notable for their contribution in social reform and economic growth. Sultans used to work for the common people and they created attractive cities for their living. They also created accommodation and area for the common people in the palace area.

The study primarily focuses on the residential, commercial and the gathering places of the medieval cities. Art and the architecture are critical elements for evaluating historical values, as well as civilizations. Thus, people, space, living pattern, interaction spaces and commercial hubs have been selected as areas of study. As the title suggests, the 'other story' refers to the analysis and identification of urbanism both within and outside the wall.

Exploring the existing literature with additional pictographic information such as historic diagrams and drawings, the study started with the potential to fill the missing parts of the statement of the particular area. A logical reconstruction of what the areas looked like during their hay day was developed based on a detailed empirical survey of the sites, pictorial information and existing literature, primarily consisting accounts of historians, voyagers and the philosophers. Through this rigorous process, spatial quality of key areas was reconstructed.

Morphology of the key spaces was analyzed to understand common settings of the medieval city; starting from the public realm to the private. Even though the imperial palaces' was analyzed, the focus was on the larger aspects of the medieval city within the fortified walls. Thus Sultanate medieval city of Gaur, pre-Mughal or the Sultanate Bengal river fort medieval city at Gaur, West Bengal, India and Bangladesh was selected. Case studies were used to unfold the scale, space, common commercial area of the city and to illustrate the gathering places of the area. Overall, the key focus of the study was to unfold the hierarchy of the spatial profile and the characteristics, ancient construction technique and the neighborhood Mohalla pattern of Sultanate Gaur of Bengal.

FIGURE 3.4: Fortified walls of Gaur
Massive thick wall of the Gaur citadel and the main palace showing the materials of construction, restoration of the walls, ruins of the inner wall with pointed arch alcove and niches and the gorgeous terracotta works of termination bands.

Source: Author

FIGURE 3.5: Ancient paintings of Gaur
Ancient painting showing the glorious ruins architecture of Gaur medieval city, painted by Sitaram (1814).

Source: British Library Images online

CHARACTERISTICS OF THE MEDIEVAL CITY OF GAUR: IN AND OUTSIDE THE WALLS

One of the shining examples, Gaur, one of the largest medieval cities in the Indian subcontinent, was the capital of Bengal from c. 1450 CE to 1565 CE (Khan, 1931; Khan, 1986). It was located on the eastern strip of land between the Ganges and the Mahananda rivers, now in present day India and Bangladesh. From the early fifteenth century, Gaur and Pandua[2] were becoming populous. Perhaps it was the pressure of population that led Sultan Nasiruddin Mahmud to shift the capital to Gaur from Pandua (Majumdar, 1971). The rise of the overseas port of Saptagram (another inland port of India) took place around the same time. Since then, the immigration to Gaur continued at a brisk pace while other towns on the Bhagirathi also began to grow, mostly acting as suppliers of textile to Saptagram and Gaur. It is significant that the city of Gaur began to grow towards the south beyond the wall, whose remains have been recently explored by a Bangladesh team.

FIGURE 3.6: Painting of Chhoto Shona mosque, Gaur
The painting shows Chhoto Shona mosque, Gaur. The painting was done by James Moffat (1775-1815 CE).

Source: British Library Images Online; Fisher, 1811

THE SPATIAL PATTERN

Gaur, the sultanate capital of Bengal, is one of the finest examples of a medieval city in the subcontinent. The city was designed with proper notion, organization and intellectual planning. The city was fortified with three layers of massive embankment, double and triple layers of battered fortress walls, where numerous ditches and designed moats or trenches were dug for defensive purposes. The natural settings also helped in making of the strategic plan brilliantly as the landscape of the area was inherently unique having dense mango gardens. The ruins of Gaur left tresses showing this area was dotted with mango gardens up to that time.

Henry Creighton[3], an indigo planter living near Gaur, gave a description of the morphology of the city in 1786 CE, including a sketch of the place and superb drawings of its monuments. He found the ruins of the city extending up to ten miles in length and one and half mile in breadth, lying between the Ganges and the Mahananda; the latter became a lagoon by the end of the fifteenth century.

COMPONENTS OF THE CITY

The city was elongated towards north and south, as the river Ganges and its main branch Mahananda was flowing from the eastern and the western bank of the region. The city took the advantage of having a river route from the twin-elongated edge of the embankment; it grew naturally having similar qualities of the 'Inland port of Bengal'. Thus, the spatial strategy was to enter from the huge gathering spaces to the smaller ones. The key components of city were the Jahajghata (boat landing terrace), the embankment, fortified walls, the triumphal gateways, the inherent topography with mango gardens, natural ditches, moats, citadels, the paved street pattern, mosques, tombs, mohallah (residential area) and the bazaar (see Figure 3.7 and 3.8).

The city had progression of spatial linkages, which can be easily identified from the peripheral embankment, where the gigantic gateways were used as thresholds. The massive thick battered walls and the embankment were used both as a path and strong edge. The streets and lanes were circulated in-between the building masses, especially through the mohallahs and the bazaars. The spatial sequence was terminated at the courtyard of the single storied dwellings.

FIGURE 3.7: Flow chart of different spatial organization
The flow chart shows different spatial organization, starting from private to public arena.

Source: Author

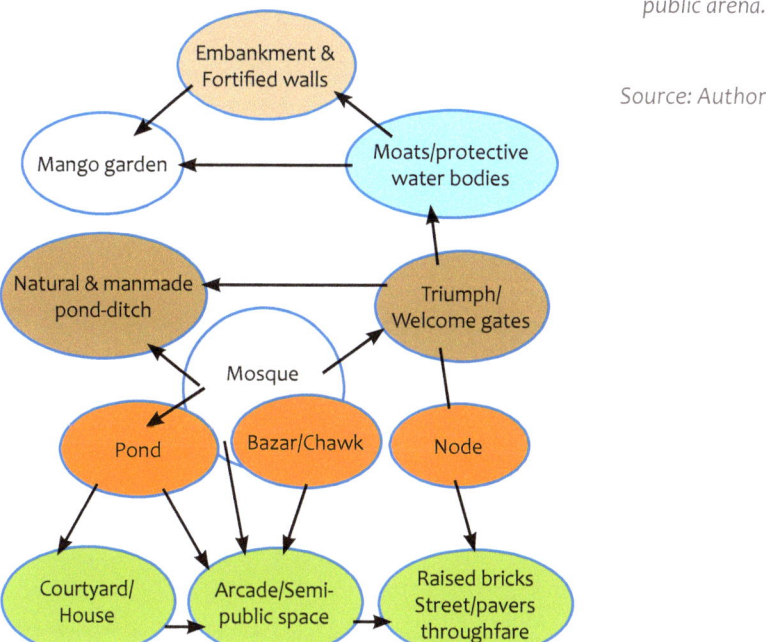

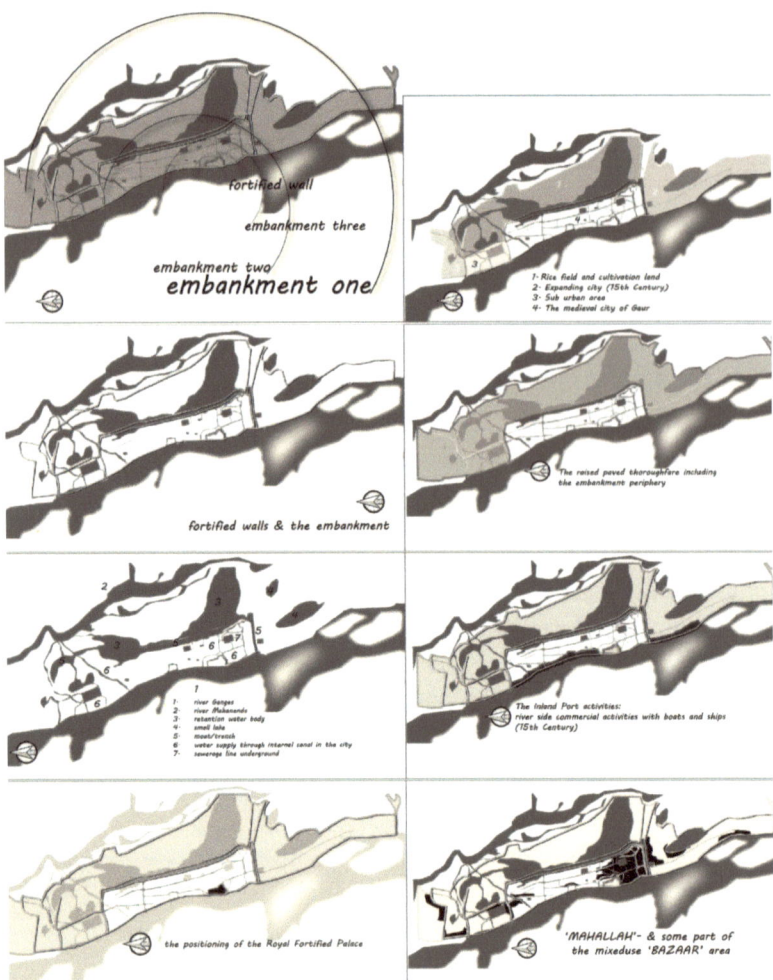

FIGURE 3.8: Evolution of Sultanate Gaur
Various stages of the spatial changes of Sultanate capital of Gaur, 1450 to 1565 CE.

Source: Author

BROAD SENSE OF SPATIAL FEATURE: STRATUM BASED ZONING

Spatial pattern and the components of the master plan of entire Gaur could be identified from the different plates respecting the stratum of the fort, surrounding context of the city, fort walls and embankment, thoroughfare pattern, moat, water and river route management, inland port activities, the palace and the citadel and lastly the residential mohallah and mixed use pattern of the city.

The first stratum was lying with in grass field that used to maintain water during the rainy season. The grass field was utilized as a cultivation field for state granary. Within this first layer of the walls, permanent water bodies remained for retention of water supply for the community (see Figure 3.8). Beyond the first stratum of the embankment and the fortification, the suburban area was developed during those days. The area happened to grow towards the northwestern and the southeastern part of the city. Basically the settlement was growing at those regions and migrants from other areas settled in the suburban area (see Figure 3.8).

In the second stratum, the embankment and the fortification used to be the effective elements. This strong line of the embankment and the fortification was running from the extreme northwestern to southeastern part and eventually was expected to expand to the southern part of the present territory of Bangladesh, where the Chhota Sona, Darasbari and Khaniadighi mosques are situated. Although the wall was turned to the sharp western face heading to the Kotwali Darwaza, the city remains show the tress of continuing its boundary further south. Especially this bracket of the embankment and the fortification used to contain deep moats in between the third one on the eastern highland. The pattern of the wall was organic or irregular because of the geographical deviation (Figure 3.8).

FIGURE 3.9: Ruins of inland port area at Phulbari

The commercial area of Gaur was connected by the moat to the river Ganges and Bhagirothi.

Source: Author

The third stratum happened to be running shortly corresponding the second one, and both the embankment and the fortification were heading towards the Kotwali Darwaza. This was associated with mosques, tombs and the commercial districts. The landscape was uniquely generated with dense mango gardens. The neighborhood pattern used to be sensitive to the natural terrain. The famous mosques and the residential Mohallah were set within this wall of the main fort-citadel. The other infrastructures were developed in between this wall. Citadel walls were dedicated to the royal palace (see Figure 3.1) and the landing terrace. This was the main protected area fortified by connecting moat with the Ganges.

At the same time, the commercial area, Phulbari (see Figure 3.9) of Gaur, had the same situation and connected with the moat at the river Ganges's side. Therefore, the main third wall is for the imperial settings only. This fortification contains the three segments on the inner side with water bodies. Apart from this, the entire area was dotted with large and small tanks; while some were dug by the sultans others were natural.

MOHALLAH WITH MOSQUE

The city had an array of beautiful mosques, most of them serving local communities. It shows that the city was developed by some groups of communities in neighborhood pattern; in Muslim term known as mohallah. Mohallah is the homogenous group of people or the community who live in a cooperative society. Often a traditional neighborhood or community could be a mohallah. In the case of Gaur, perhaps mohallahs generated centered around mosques, as the mosque was the administrative hub for the state of sultanate society and society used to emerge with a mosque. Mosque served multiple purposes during the sultanate period; such as governing center and forum of the society and educational facilities, congregation space for prayer as well as other Islamic festivals. Besides this, a coexistence of religious rituals was part of the society. It is noticeable that during the sultanate period, many Hindu brick temples were erected and the people from other religions could perform their rituals and festivals. Husain Shah's long reign (1494–1519 CE) of more than a quarter of a century was a period of peace and prosperity, which was strikingly in contrast to the period, that preceded it. The liberal attitude of Husain Shah towards his Hindu subjects is also an important feature of his reign (Majumdar, 2006). According to a contemporary Vaisnava poet,

FIGURE 3.10: Mohallah of Sultanate Capital of Gaur
Conjectural restoration sketch showing the different stages and the arenas of structures, especially the components of a Mohallah.

Source: Author

Sultan Alauddin Hussain Shah saw a procession led by *Chaitannya* (1486–1534 CE)[4] on the opposite bank of the river.

Generally mohallahs evolved with a group of artisans who shared a profession, such as *tanti* (weavers), potter, goldsmith, blacksmith, sculptor or craftsman, and carpenters. In the medieval city of Gaur these mohallahs used to group together. The mohallah had some common characteristics, the entrance of the residential units used to be seated just on the winding lane or the street. Some mohallahs contained small nodal point or square where important commercial transaction used to take place. Generally the nodes of adjacent mohallahs were interconnected. Mohallah contained a cluster of houses with mosque, bazaar, courtyards, etc. The spine streets or the lanes provided connectivity in-between the residences of mohallahs, this pattern prevailed in Gaur. Archaeological evidences from the site shows moderate density of the mohallah where the localities used to live in the southern part of the citadel of the palace wall.

Local legends identified the high area south of the citadel, from where Buddhist and Hindu icons have been found, as the commercial centre of Gaur. Traditionally it is termed Lal Bazaar, while a section of it is called Mahajan Tola. Cowries and coarse pottery were found in profusion in the area contiguous to the citadel and from one mile in a square area. The ruins indicate the existence of several mohallahs or wards dating from pre-Islamic days (Ray, 1995).

POPULATION AND DENSITY

The city seems to have been densely populated. Antorio de Britto, Portuguese interpreter in 1521 CE, speaks of a high population density. He found it difficult to move through the crowded streets while the nobles used to employ a number of retainers to clear the way. Fariya Y Sousa (Portuguese historian of seventeen century)[5], and following him others, put the number of inhabitants at twelve lacs while the visiting Frenchman put the population at forty thousand hearth. Taking five persons per family, the population would come to two lacs, quite close to two lac twenty thousand of contemporary Fathepur Sikri. The population density of Gaur would however be over two thousand persons per square mile in an eighty square mile area. The analysis of revenue data, given by Abul Fazl[6] in 1595-96 CE, obviously based on earlier revenue figures, gives an idea of the tremendous draw of the Gaur area and its high population density.

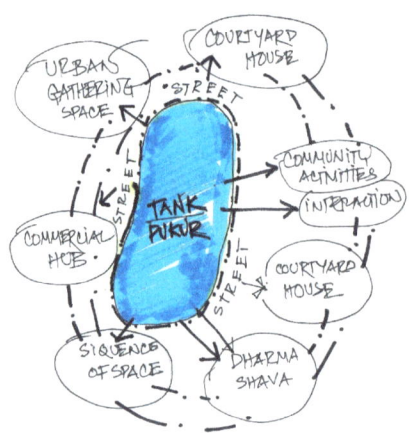

FIGURE 3.11: Spatial relationship of tank with adjacent functions
Gaur city was dotted with ditch and small tanks. Naturally, house forms often generated along the edge of the tanks; mostly these were indigenous constructions.

Source: Author

CHARACTERISTICS OF THE DWELLINGS: SCALE, PROPORTION AND STREET–FAÇADE RELATIONSHIP

The medieval city Gaur today is the ruins of brilliant historic mosque, tombs, triumphal gateways, and undoubtedly this city was colorful from its origin. The religious buildings of Gaur were colored with enameled tiles, entire mosques were enveloped with beautiful blue, sap green, yellow ocred and white designed motif. Several structures still bear witness of the grandeur; they include the Gumti Gate (see Figure 3.1), Latin Mosque, Chika Mosque and few in Dakhil Darwaza. It has been proven by many other Chinese and Portuguese voyagers and Bengali Vaishnavas that the Gaur city was charming with colorful and fabulous architecture. At the same time the city was getting popular also, perhaps it was during the reign of the Sultan Hussain Shahi (1494-1519 CE). Secular or peoples' architecture during those days was not mundane. Most of the mohallahs were vibrant with people as Gaur city was highly populated. Bazaar or the commercial area was lively with transactions. The streets headed (see Figure 3.11) towards the entrance of the courtyard house; Gaur city was dotted with ditch and small tanks. Naturally, house forms often generated along the edge of the tanks, mostly these were indigenous constructions.

Along the streets, single storied and low height dwelling form developed with courtyard. Apart from this, blue and yellow ocred color dominated enameled tiles (see Figure 3.14). Single storied low houses were developed, most of these dwellings belonged to the well-off families. The basic material used were small square thin brick terracotta. The red thin bricks had enamel coating and in other cases tiles were used.

In some cases, the columns of the dwellings were made with solid logs from trees. On the other hand, in the Darbar hall monolithic columns were used. Elaborate roofing patterns were not generally used in the residential units, but it may have been usual to cast roofs with rafters, purlins, wooden joist and bamboo in deep intervals. Although during the sultanate period dome-making artisanship had some achievements, until then for the residential roofing terracotta flat and in some cases curved tiles were preferred. To make the roofing compressive and strong, narrow brick vaulting in the inner side of the roof was used. The dwellings were interactive with the streets.

Innovative tiles work on the floor excavated by DOA, Bangladesh in 2002, of the Chhoto Shona mosque, (1529 CE) during the reign of Hussain Shahi, 1494-1519 CE. This type of tiles was used in the residential units of the mohallah; many tourists from the ancient period describe the house floor being colored with different enamel tiles.

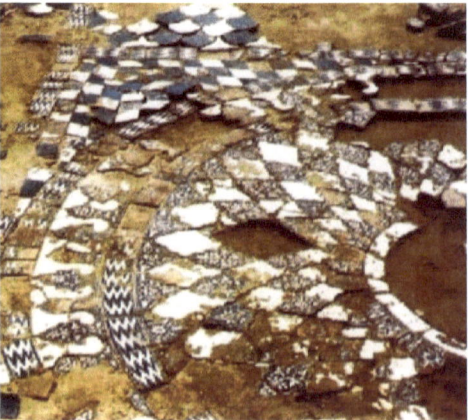

FIGURE 3.12: Ornamental tiles of Gaur
Innovative golden and bluish tiles work on the floor excavated by DOA, Bangladesh in 2002 of Chhoto Shona mosque.

Source: Author

Castenhada de Lopez[7] (Portuguese historian) left a description of the houses. The buildings were low-lying, wrought with golden and bluish tiles (see Figure 3.12) and they had numerous courtyards and gardens. The floors of each house were covered with ornamental tiles. Humayun's companion, author of the *Waquiyat-i Mustaqui* (Ray, 1995), stated that Humayun was struck by the Chinese tiles, which were used on the floors as well as the walls of the rooms. There is no mention of any double-storied house at Gaur, although the Portuguese interpreter has described the underground room of the Darbar hall. Between the citadel and the eastern embankment, a ruined structure, supposed to be the house of a legendary merchant, Chand Saudagar, has been identified as the Belbari Madrasa, the only one found so far within the walled city. The raised land on both sides of the canal from the Belbari Madrasa to the west, where fine ceramics have been found, would suggest that it was an area inhabited by upper class people. The frontal area of the land gradually slopes down to the canal. The area from the Chhota Sagar Dighi to

FIGURE 3.13: Sultanate bricks
6.5" × 6.5" × 1.75" Sultanate Bricks, the main module for building mosque, house, bridge, paved walkway etc.

Source: Author

FIGURE 3.14: Diagrammatic analysis showing hierarchy of spaces
The figure shows interaction of the structure, scale, volume typology of the house pattern and the commercial areas etc. The scale, proportion, sense of enclosure and the mass volume are analyzed.

Source: Author

the eastern embankment seems to have been occupied by marginal people as no ruins or artifacts have been found.

THOROUGHFARE PATTERN

The streets were paved with red bricks (see Figure 3.13) and comparatively elevated from the ground level. The streets were hierarchy based, the first layer street, the second layer street, the third was the winding-narrow one and the fourth one was the embankment peripheral street. According to the master plan the major avenue was elongated towards north-south. The other streets were connected in various patterns.

The city had two large paved roads, parallel to the river, in the north-south direction, crisscrossed by smaller lanes and canals, some of which still exist. The first layer streets usually passed by the long distance areas; citadel, tombs and mosques were located on this street.

The second layer was executed with the connection of two parallel primary streets, several connections created a network. Basically mohallah used to start through this second layer of the street, with commercial activities or bazaar on both sides as the common form. Usually nodal points or mosques would be at the intersection point of two secondary streets. Gaur had winding narrow lanes that passed through densely populated residential areas, as confirmed by historical references. The embankment worked as the primary infrastructure, the entire fortified walls were ringed with the embankment street as well as the encampment chain or the regimented chain.

The Portuguese found the streets well mapped out and arranged. Certain types of goods, such as weapons, sweetmeats or food, were sold on separate streets, similar to other large medieval cities of the Indian subcontinent. The Portuguese favorably compared this city with Lisbon.

CONCLUSION

Analyzing the narration and statements of historical scholars, the study attempts to unfold some primary information which would possibly facilitate further research in the field. The study attempts to explore the following topics:

- Segmental spatial pattern of the strategic master plan,
- Innovative ancient or Sultanate construction technique,
- Social structure and sequential place for the people,
- Ornamentation on terracotta walls and other elements used on walls for beautification,
- Floor finish and understanding of materials for both secular and religious structures,

- Plumbing, water supply and sewerage history of the city,
- Brick module and layering on enamel tiles.

Mohallah, how it was and the cluster of the dense residential structure of the Gaur medieval city, was unique compared to the other Islamic medieval cities around the world. The elaboration was done through conjectural restoration. The study expresses the hierarchy of the spatial profile both for public and private realm through illustration. Political instabilities and water resource management became vital issues behind the decline of Gaur. The city was designed with full of brilliance and intellectual thought. People and cultural co-existence were exemplary in the city, especially during the reign of the Hussain Shahi. Power, mightiness, fortress formula and at the same time infrastructural facilities for the city people and inhabitants were significant achievements. Tourists and philosophers around the world visited the city and left several accounts with many appreciations and comments regarding Gaur. The study attempts to address some of the notations and narrative information through technical and critical point of view to justify the ambiance and the spatial quality within and outside the city. The mohallah has been analyzed based on field survey and literature review primarily accounts of reputed voyagers. The voyagers who used to visit the city were from different disciplines and backgrounds. Commonalities of statements were picked up for analyzing the site and the city.

Lastly,
Civilization begins with order, grows with liberty, and dies with chaos…
– Will Durant

ENDNOTES

1. The Mamluk Style (1298-1313). The Early Illyas Shahi Style (1352-1414).The Eklakhi Style (1414-14). The latter Illyas Shahi Style (1435-1487). The Khan-E-Jahan Style (Regional Style 14th century). Hussain Shahi Style (1494-1538)
2. Pandua was the Sultanate capital of Muslim Bengal in 1338 and 1500 AD
3. From *Views at Gaur*, six aquatints by James Moffat after Henry Creighton, published by Moffat in Calcutta 1808. Henry Creighton (UK, 1767-1807) (Creighton, 1817)
4. Chaitanya Mahaprabhu is revered by devotees as an incarnation of Krishna and Radharani as avatars of the *Parmatma*, or Supreme Godhead. He was born in a Bengali Hindu family. According to *Chaitanya*

Charitamruta, *Nimāi* was born on the full moon night of 18 February 1486, at the time of a lunar eclipse

5. Manuel de Faria e Sousa (18 March 1590 – 3 June 1649) was a Portuguese historian and poet, frequently writing in Spanish (Asher, 1984).
6. Shaikh Abu al-Fazal ibn Mubarak also known as Abu'l-Fazl, Abu'l Fadl and Abu'l-Fadl 'Allami (January 14, 1551 – August 12, 1602) was the vizier of the great Mughal emperor Akbar, and author of the *Akbarnama*, the official history of Akbar's reign in three volumes, (the third volume is known as the *Ain-i-Akbari*) and a Persian translation of the Bible. He was also one of the Nine Jewels (Hindi: Navaratnas) of Akbar's royal court and the brother of Faizi, the poet laureate of Emperor Akbar (Grover, 1996).
7. Fernão Lopes de Castaneda (Santarém, c. 1500 - Coimbra, 1559) was a historian Portuguese in rebirth. His *History of the Discovery and Conquest of India by the Portuguese*, which stands for the abundance of geographic and ethnographic objective information, was widely translated throughout Europe.

REFERENCES

- Ahmed, A. S. M. (2006). *Mosque Architecture in Bangladesh*. Dhaka: UNESCO
- Ahmed, N. (1980). *Islamic Heritage of Bangladesh*. Dacca: Padma Printers.
- Ahmed, N. (1984). *Discover the monuments of Bangladesh*: University Press.
- Asher, C. B. (1984). Inventory of key monuments. *The Islamic Heritage of Bengal*. Paris.
- British Library Images Online. from http://imagesonline.bl.uk/index.php?service=search&action=do_quick_search&language=en&q=%2320362
- Brown, P. (2013). *Indian architecture (the Islamic period)*: Read Books Ltd.
- Creighton, H. (1817). *The Ruins of Gaur*.
- Cunningham, A. (1882). *Archaeological Survey of India Reports (Vol. XV)*. Calcutta: Office of the Superintendent of Government Printing.
- Dani, A. H. (1961). *Muslim Architecture in Bengal*. Dacca.
- Fisher, T. (1811). A map of Gour [Gaur], 1801. Retrieved 25 August, 2017, from http://www.bl.uk/onlinegallery/onlineex/apac/other/019wzz000003481u00019000.html
- Frishman, M., & Khan, H. U. (2002). *The Mosque*. London: Thames and Hudson Ltd.
- Grover, S. (1996). *Islamic architecture in India*: South Asia Books.

- Hasan, P. (2007). *Sultans and Mosques, the Early Muslim Architecture of Bangladesh*: IB Tauris.
- Hasan, S. M. (1979). *Mosque architecture of pre-Mughal Bengal*. Dhaka: UPL.
- Husain, A. Y. (2015, 4 March). Munim Khan Khan-i-Khanan. Retrieved 25 August, 2017, from http://en.banglapedia.org/index.php?title=Munim_Khan_Khan-i-Khanan
- Hussain, A. B. M. (1996). Some observations on the development of Gawr-Lakhnawti and its monuments. *Journal of Bengal Art*, 1, 173-178.
- Karim, A. (2015, 16 March). Shah Shuja. Retrieved 25 August, 2017, from http://en.banglapedia.org/index.php?title=Shah_Shuja
- Khan, A. A. (1931). *Memoirs of Gaur and Pandua*. Calcutta.
- Khan, M. (1986). *Memoirs of Gaur and Pandua* (H. Stapleton Ed.). Calcutta
- Majumdar, D. R. C. (1971). *History of Ancient Bengal*. Kolkata: Tulshi Prakashani.
- Majumdar, R. C. (2006). *The Delhi Sultanate*. Mumbai: Bharatiya Vidya Bhavan.
- Ravenshaw, J. H., Ravenshaw, C., & Blochmann, H. (1878). *Gaur, Its Ruins and Inscriptions*: C. Kegan Paul.
- Ray, A. (1995). Archaeological Reconnaissance at the City of Gaur–A Preliminary Report. *Pratna Sameeksha*, 2-3, 245-263.
- Tadgell, C. (2002). *The History of Architecture in India*. Singapore: Phaidon Press.

FIGURE 4.1: Exterior of House 5
The semi-open verandah at ground level facing north providing a buffer from the street at entry.

Source: Author

LEARNING FROM PANAM NAGAR: LESSONS FROM THE TRANSITIONAL BRITISH COLONIAL HYBRID HOUSES

Iftekhar Ahmed
Badruzzahan Ahmed

INTRODUCTION

Panam Nagar (also known as *Painam*) is a linear township of fortynine abandoned street-front houses once owned by rich Hindu merchants of the British colonial era. It is located at Sonargaon, former capital of Bengal during the Sultanate Period. Sonargaon originated during the later half of the thirteenth century as a Sultanate capital, which was later captured by the Mughal in 1611 (Ahmed, 1993; Khan, 2014). Currently, it falls under Narayanganj district of Bangladesh, 29 km northeast of Dhaka. As a township of the Hindu elite, Panam Nagar flourished in the late 19th and early 20th century as a trading and cultural hub due to the trading activities (purchase of muslin and other cotton fabrics) of the British East India company (Hussain, 1997, 2007; Kaderi, 1998). The town continued to prosper till the partition of Indian subcontinent in 1947. Having once been a thriving locality, most of these houses were abandoned in the 1960s after local riots broke out following the partition of the Indian subcontinent in 1947. Few owners who continued to stay, left after the Liberation War of Bangladesh in 1971, vacating Panam Nagar entirely. Locals then illegally occupied Panam Nagar from the 1970s until 2004. Due to lack of maintenance or restoration for over three decades, the heritage township became vulnerable.

Under the circumstances, the government of Bangladesh declared the town an archaeological site in March 2003; and the 49 houses, on more than 10 acres of land, were marked as part of an archaeological site for protection and conservation (Panam Nagar declared archeological site, 2003). Panam Nagar was taken over by the Department of Archaeology of the Ministry of Cultural Affairs, under the Antiquities Act 1968 (The Antiquities Act, 1968). Subsequently, the illegal occupants were evicted by the government. In 2005-2006 fiscal year, the Department of Archaeology undertook a Tk 5 crore (US$ 700,000 approximately) conservation project for Panam Nagar which was to be completed by June 2007. Under this project 16 buildings underwent restoration work at various degrees (Ali, 2007). However, the works were halted when the civil society and citizens protested that the restoration were insensitive to the original style, unskilled and damaged the buildings rather than protecting them. In 2008, Panam Nagar was listed in the *2008 Watch List of the 100 Most Endangered Sites* by the World Monuments Fund (Evarts, 2007).

During its heyday, it is estimated that about 1400 families of Hindu and Muslim weavers lived in and around Panam (Khan, 2014). A select group of Hindu merchant–talukdars, who were favored by the British, chose the site of the present township for their residence.

FIGURE 4.2: Street front houses of Panam Nagar
The buildings were built in the physical, climatic and social context of Bengal under European influence.

Source: Author

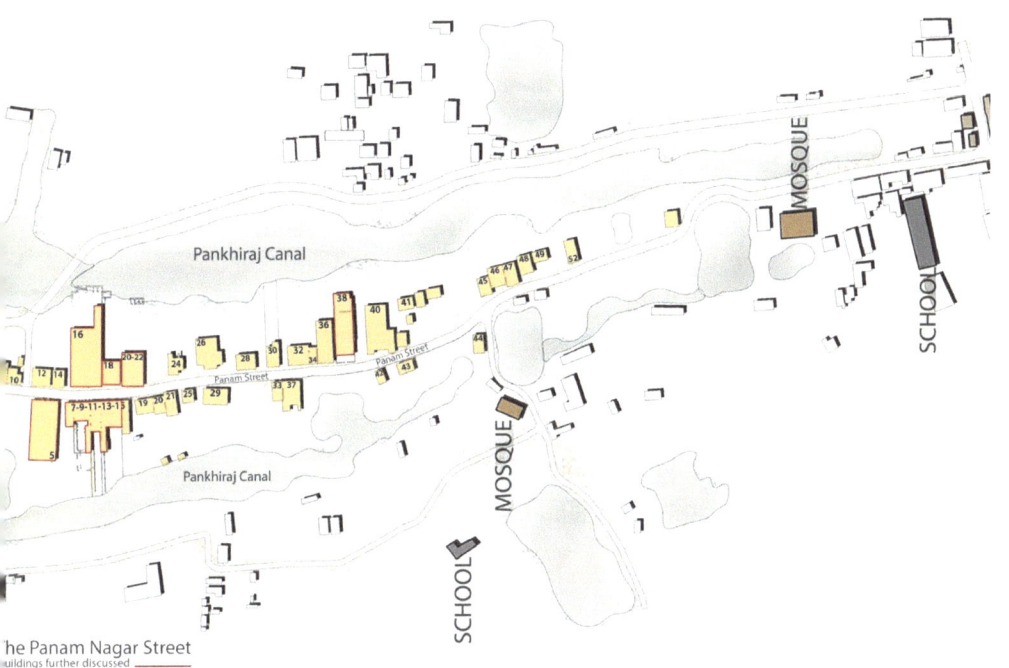

FIGURE 4.3: Plan showing hybrid houses of Panam Nagar
The entire settlement is on a flat site stretched on both sides of a single five meter street about 0.6 km long. An artificial canal runs all around the township.

Source: Author

Few residences date back to early nineteenth and most of the others to late nineteenth and early twentieth century (see Figure 4.2). Although several buildings of Panam Nagar can be traced back to the Mughal Period by style, the physical features of most buildings can be categorized under British Colonial style (Ahmed, 1984; Khan, 2014; Khatun, 2006). The Hindu merchants visited Europe for trade purposes regularly and were exposed to then avant-garde architecture of Europe (Ahmed, 2014; Ahmed, 1986; Roy, 1891; Sarkar, 1948). Thus, the street-front facades display strong European influences in architectural features such as Corinthian columns, pilasters, decorated friezes and arched openings often blended with local motifs (Brown, 1956; Grover, 1981; Mowla & Reza, 2000).

However, it is important to note that these buildings were built in the physical, climatic and social context of Bengal under European influence by the then political and affluent rulers of the region. This hybrid aspect is reflected in architecture and planning of the buildings, where the exterior shows strong European influence while the interior spaces is adapted from the local vernacular spatial layout of Bengal region. Typical vernacular homesteads of Bengal had living quarters which were arranged around an open to sky courtyard. This feature is repeated in several buildings of Panam Nagar. However, a significant variation is that the majority of courtyards of Panam Nagar is covered, more similar to European style double-height hall rooms. Additionally, the buildings also have a semi-open circulation space that acted as an intermediate space between the living quarters and the courtyard. Most of the buildings have a slightly elevated porch space, usually with decorated openings towards the street that precedes this internal arrangement.

In terms of architecture and town planning, Panam Nagar is one of its kind in Bangladesh. No other location in the region has such a township with so many heritage buildings that survived together as a group. Thus, the architectural and historical significance of Panam Nagar has always been deemed important for the history of the region, and as of today, this remains the most discussed aspect of Panam Nagar (Ahmed, 2006, 2007). Yet, this strong focus on the image of heritage township has shadowed another major aspect that has been rarely explored in the study of Panam Nagar. While the existing studies and records document the physical (Shaikh & Rahman, 2009) and historical aspects (Ali, 1990; Taylor, 1840; Wise, 1874) of Panam Nagar, there are almost no study of how social aspects of life shaped architectural spaces of Panam Nagar. In several cases, it could have been the other way around, as one has no idea how these hybrid structures must have affected the everyday lives of its occupants. This study aims to address this unexplored area: the social impacts of architectural and planning features of Panam Nagar.

PHYSICAL SPACES OF PANAM NAGAR: SOCIOCULTURAL INFLUENCES

The vernacular housing form of the region is generally a compact or semi-compact form around an open to sky courtyard. Each function not only faces the courtyard, it also has a strong relationship with immediate hierarchical spaces they surround. This form finds its place in Panam Nagar in myriad of interpreted forms rarely directly replicating its origin. A close examination of the plans reveals that the hybrid houses of Panam Nagar meet a specific need to separate the varying degrees of public and private domains in the hierarchy of spaces. The dialogue is subtle, open to interpretation, but always effective. The varying proportion of spaces attributed to serve this purpose range from highly lavish to very compact housing forms. However, the dialogue is equally successful in each case.

The entire settlement is on a flat site stretched on both sides of a single five-meter street about 0.6 km long. An artificial canal runs all around the township (see Figure 4.3). The building heights vary from single to three stories. Most of the urban street front houses can be categorized into three basic types: central courtyard type, central hall type and houses without hall or court. In most cases the central space (hall or court) is the center of the houses, often extensively decorated and celebrated with good visual and physical access. The building layouts clusters around a paved open to sky courtyard where every day social activities took place. In general, the courtyards are surrounded by semi-open veranda on all or most sides. The houses without court or halls are mostly single storied. There is a unity among the variety of languages which has been achieved with volume, height, symmetry, arched openings in the entry façade, etc. The wide array of veranda, balcony, loggia, and porch provides the variety according to person requirements of the owners.

The houses are typically rectangular, both detached and attached types, and elongated in the north-south direction. The rectangular form and proportions tend to follow several important aspects, the character of the lot they are based on, their dialogue with the neighbors and how they open to the street and back yard which was the heart of the social and private life in the township. The layout shows extensive use of backyard facilities among the adjoining houses with steps of yards, leading to shared pond, *ghat*, well etc. This indicates a close social relationship among neighbors. The size, dimensions and shape of the covered courts or relationship with the neighbor and street determined the orientation and size of the opening which are gathered on the important facades that speak of the social relationship and intro-extrovert nature of these houses at the same time. They range from French windows to regular windows. The openings on the streets are almost naturally highly interactive and establish a strong dialogue with the street. The width and height of the open and covered courtyards determine the amount of light allowed in the adjacent rooms. The decision of placing windows above a certain level follows the considerations of privacy while at other spaces they are more liberal, allowing ample light into more public spaces and inviting social interaction. The layering of spaces has a close relationship with the selection of windows.

EXPLORING THE MISSING LINK IN THE LOCAL HOUSING FORM AND SPACE

The development of urban housing in this part of Bengal is about two to three hundred years old. During the Mughal era, the homesteads of the region were predominantly rural having similar spatial layouts, choice of materials and physical expressions such as elevations, openings, decorations, etc. After the arrival of the Europeans in the Indian subcontinent, the homesteads evolved due to external foreign influences during the late 17th to early 20th century, primarily during the British colonial era. Houses from this period were generally inspired from their rural vernacular counterpart, mostly clustered around courtyards.

While the rural housing formation of Bengal is the product of a thousand years of evolution where form and space has an almost instinctive, natural relationship and dialogue, the hybrid houses of Panam Nagar stand on a unique ground. Even though inspired from affluent European villas in many aspects, the soul of these houses is safely grounded in local society, culture and climate. Another important issue here is, unlike their rural counterpart, the growth is not incremental, these are complete constructions reflecting the choice that the designer/owner found best suits their purpose. The Hindu traders were affluent but possibly without political power. This dichotomy is reflected in the houses which have a vernacular layout with only its street-front façades having European influences. It appears as if the Hindu merchants were somehow trying to display their financial status, through the expression of architectural features copied from their colonial rulers, yet was unable to give-up their contextual ways of living entirely which is reflected in the spatial layout that is more vernacular and regional. Overall, the functional requirements of that particular era were met where the rich owners found suitable interpretations of the rural housing formation that successfully justified the need of society, culture and climate.

Even though the early urban houses show the inspiration and influences of the rural vernacular, more recent examples (from the last three to four decades) show there has been a missing link in the evolution of local housing form. The urban houses of present day Bangladesh (in areas such as Dhanmondi, Gulshan, etc. of Dhaka city) seem very different from its rural predecessors and somehow more similar to housing of the European or Western world. The current housing practice highly relies on alien foreign examples, resulting in an array of contemporary housing form devoid of any relation or relevance to local context. There are very few urban residential buildings in Bangladesh that exist as examples of the transitional phase where urban form interpreted the rural displaying a shift from contextual to foreign influences. Panam Nagar is one of those rare intermediary examples of residences in an urban township that shows the evolution. Studying Panam Nagar from a social perspective could provide the missing link between the above described discrepancies.

The study contests that some elements of culture remain unchanged (such as the need for privacy at various spaces), despite the changing environments. It is these elements that are of particular interest of this study as they stand the test of time and shows why the design solutions can be still valid for today. The township showcases a significant part of the historical evolution of local housing typology with adapted spaces having their own social meaning. With an aim to explore the socio-cultural significance of architectural and urban spaces of Panam Nagar, social interpretation of the physical spaces, how the creation of these spaces reflects the occupants' mind-set and society in a transitional time of the Bengal region, the physical spaces have been analyzed in terms of their original functions as well as whether the interpreted space typology has a relevance today. It also explores the interpreted space typologies that resulted from hybridization of Bengal's local adaptations with European influences (as an expression of political aspirations) in terms of architectural expressions during the transitional period of housing form that Panam Nagar exhibits.

The lessons from the hybrid houses will potentially enhance the knowledge base of evolution of local housing and may contribute to creating livable middle/low income dwelling environments that is rooted in local culture, society and climate. Each selected case studies present a strong case where the cultural forces were the primary determinants of the housing form.

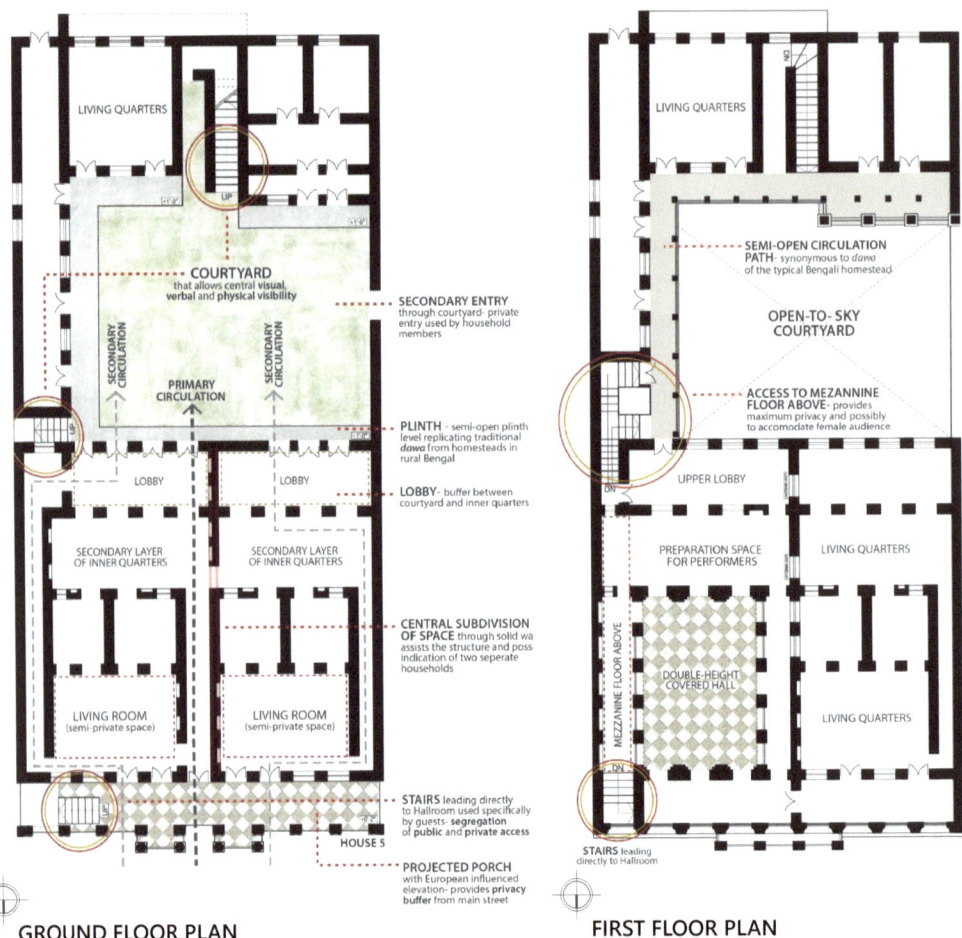

FIGURE 4.4: Plans of House 5 showing various zones and circulation
Oriented to north-south, the layout is introvert in nature, showing layering of space for privacy and climatic purpose.

Source: Author

CASE STUDIES
HOUSE 5
Orientation, circulation and zoning

House 5 is a two-storied courtyard type building (see Figure 4.1 and 4.4). Oriented to north-south, the layout is introvert in nature. It shows layering of space for privacy and climatic purpose. The semi-open verandah at ground level facing north provides a buffer from the street at entry. The two possible living rooms have series of full length openings which were either doors or windows. This provides a great deal of flexibility for the users. Between the outdoor and inner quarters there is a semi-open cloistered/arcaded space providing a buffer zone.

It is possible that the entrance portico was a later addition to highlight the entry probably to serve desired functions or changed taste. There are 3 circulation paths from the street-facing space to the rear courtyard. All 3 corridors lead to the same spaces that act as lobbies adjacent to the courtyard. There are two stairs visually connected to the courtyard.

All the architectural spaces and construction indicate a single residence, even though the clear subdivision by circulation in the middle shows there was provision for two separate users. The central subdivision of space is functional as well as structural as the span is too big for the ceiling of a brick structure in the late nineteenth century.

Privacy through layering of space and entry
The projected porch defines the main entrance in plan and volume while the secondary entry through the courtyard is subtler to provide privacy. There are traces of 3 entries accessible from the porch and an L-shaped stair at the east end that leads to the hall room on the first floor. The entry is layered for separation of public and private spaces physically and visually.

The hall room on the upper floor signifies status and upper class decadence. The double height hall room is dynamic in nature. Used on special occasions only, this selective public space is approached indirectly through stairs, once from the street side and another from the courtyard at the rear. While at ground level the corridor is fully enclosed for privacy, on the first floor it is semi-open, providing a visual link with the exterior. On the first floor, the corridor opens into a small lounge which works as a preparation space for the ballroom with the adjacent room on the south was probably used as a preparation space for performers/dancers. This layout favored privacy of both performers and guests as the small lounge offered a perfect buffer between the preparation and the performance space. The preparation space could be accessed through the central staircase adjacent to the courtyard as well. This provided flexibility for users, as on certain occasions it was necessary for the privacy of the performers/guests.

Courtyard as connector
Typically, rural vernacular houses of the Bengal region are single storied with a few having an upper floor which is accessed through a straight flight of stairs. Here the courtyard successfully adapts its rural vernacular counterpart where the adjacent spaces are semi-open, replicating the rural semi-open shaded space (locally known as *dawa*) adjoining courtyard and inner quarters. The large courtyard is private and enclosed with a single storied wall at west that has the secondary entrance. This provides full privacy for the inner spaces of the house and the space could be used for services supporting the kitchen, etc. The introvert nature of the layout suggests all the supporting services such as washing, cutting, etc., took place in the courtyard and the space was actively used.

An important feature to note is that the spatial arrangement of this house propagates from the large rear courtyard. This is unique in Panam Nagar as most houses that have hall rooms almost always has adjoining spaces propagating from the position of the hall room. Also, the courtyard is of a much larger scale compared to any other house on the Panam Street.

The semi-open spaces surrounding the courtyard are very intimate in nature, easy to access from any point as their rural origin suggests, providing room for greater social interaction. The spaces on the upper level adjacent to the courtyard are semi-open corridors or verandah providing a visual link. With instant physical access through the two staircases at the west and north, it was easy for the users to communicate visually, verbally and physically when required.

HOUSE 13-11-9-7
Asymmetric plan and lack of hierarchy of room sizes
Unlike most other houses of Panam Nagar, the circulation elements and the rooms/spaces are placed asymmetrically (see Figure 4.5 and 4.6), generally towards the periphery of each house. This is rare in Panam Nagar. The peripheral circulation has created an awkward sequence of spaces in several spots where a room can only be entered through another rather than from a common space. On the other hand, the layout has a clear circulation where the corridors are connected to staircases both physically and visually. This may have been due to personal choice or requirements. The combined circulation pattern of the four adjacent houses shows a clear break from the strong influence of European/Mughal symmetric layouts.

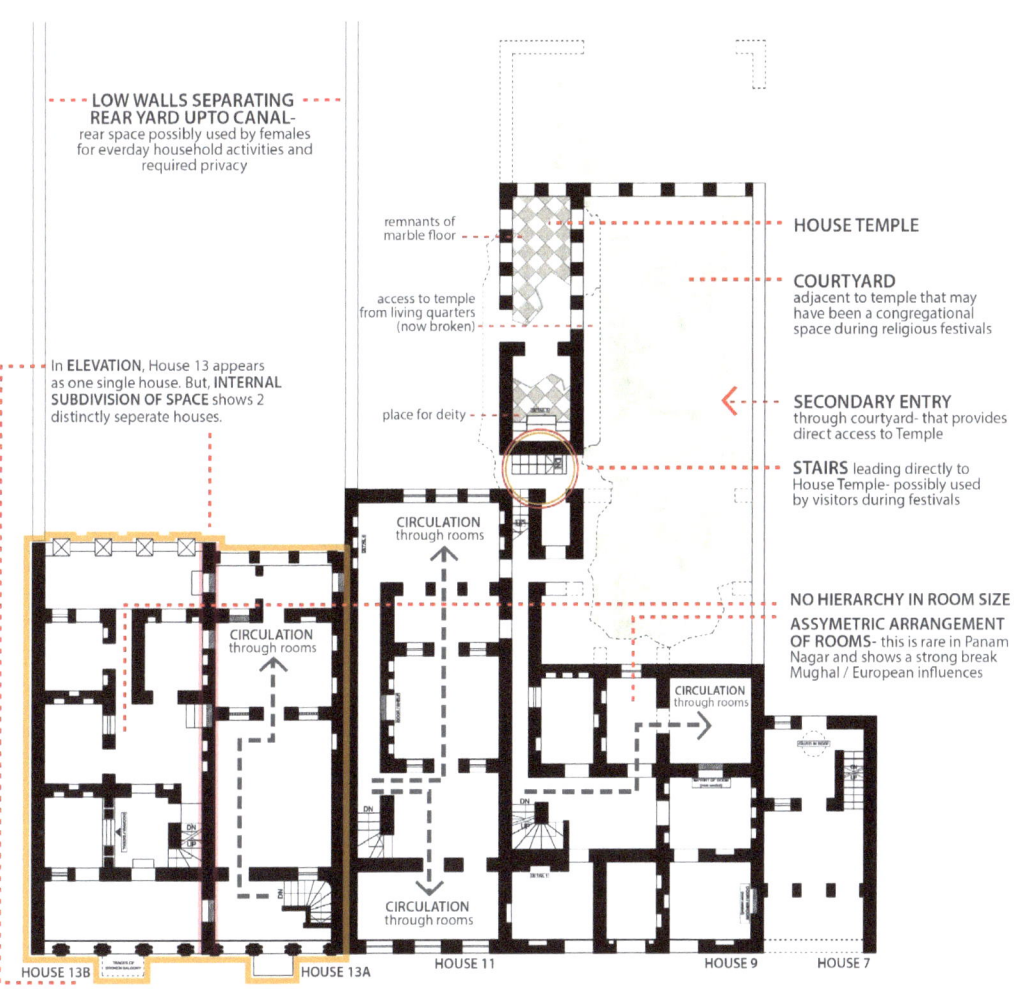

FIGURE 4.5: Plan of Houses 13-11-9-7 showing various zones and circulation

The circulation elements and the rooms/spaces are placed asymmetrically, generally towards the periphery of each house.

Source: Author

LEARNING FROM PANAM NAGAR | 63

FIGURE 4.6: Exterior of Houses 13-11-9-7
The combined circulation pattern of the four adjacent houses shows a clear break from the strong influence of European/Mughal symmetric layouts.

Source: Author

Most of the other houses of Panam Nagar reveal that a certain pattern of hierarchy was maintained in the layout of rooms and spaces; generally getting larger to smaller towards the inner quarters based on public to private uses. However, in the case of this set of buildings, the room sizes follow no hierarchy and several of them are rather equally sized. The rooms are almost square in shape and very small compared to the other buildings of the township. The layout gives the impression that use of the spaces were more moderate, barely fulfilling the requirements of accommodation.

When seen in elevation, House No. 13 appears as one integrated house. However, the internal spatial layout shows that they are two distinctly separate houses (13A-13B). A possible reason for this may be property division between family members, or an attempt to maintain a unified façade by close-knit neighbors or family members.

Articulation of religious space with regular spaces
House No. 9 has a space/room on the second floor, which was most probably used as a house temple. Although now in ruins and inaccessible without external means (ladder, etc.), there are conclusive evidences from the remnants of the structure that this space was once an integrated part of the whole house. House temples were a common practice among the Hindu elite during those days. However, the clever articulation of the temple with the rest of the house needs to be appreciated. The house temple has an adjacent courtyard on the ground level with a secondary entry from the east. It can be deduced that this space might have acted as a forecourt/congregational space during important puja festivals, providing access to non-household members. This claim can be further supported by the presence of a staircase placed right beside the temple which might have led people into the temple. This temple still has the original marble floor and the decorated miniature alter where the deity was placed.

Party walls separating back yards all the way to the canal
The set of houses 9 to 13 has their backyards separated by distinct low walls that run all the way to the *Pankhiraj* canal. This shows that although the community was evidently close knit having shared walls, roof terraces and common spaces between clusters of buildings, some degree of privacy (for the females) was still maintained, especially for access to service areas for as bathing, washing, etc. The separated backyards show that the spaces within the houses propagated from the most public spaces placed closest to the central spinal road (*dawas*, halls, etc.) to the most private spaces placed towards the canal (spaces for washing, cooking, etc.).

Hybridization with Mughal and European features
The set of houses shows strong hybridization of late Mughal and early Colonial features; showing a strong manifestation of desire to replicate the colonial rulers while keeping with the local (in this case Mughal) taste. It is one of the rare examples where one can find physical evidence of the transformation between the two successive and distinct architectural styles. The hybridization is clever, avoiding direct copy of either style rather attempting to capture a neoclassical style having adapted features of both. Elements of the front facade include pointed arches and slender, low relief columns portraying a more Mughal character than European. Most probably the hybridization belonged to the phase where the amalgamation of the two styles found a refined form. Even though the internal layout

followed the Colonial style, Mughal features are dominant in the external facade.

HOUSE 16-18-20-22
Symmetrical layout and circulation

The symmetry in circulation was probably inspired by European influences of grand symmetrical arrangement as seen in Victorian/Renaissance residences or public buildings. However, this also serves the contextual purpose of segregating circulation for privacy. It can

FIGURE 4.7: Axonometric view of Houses 16-18-20-22 showing layering of space
The courtyard is placed at the back of the building as opposed to centrally, providing secondary access to house no. 16 from adjacent spaces.

Source: Author

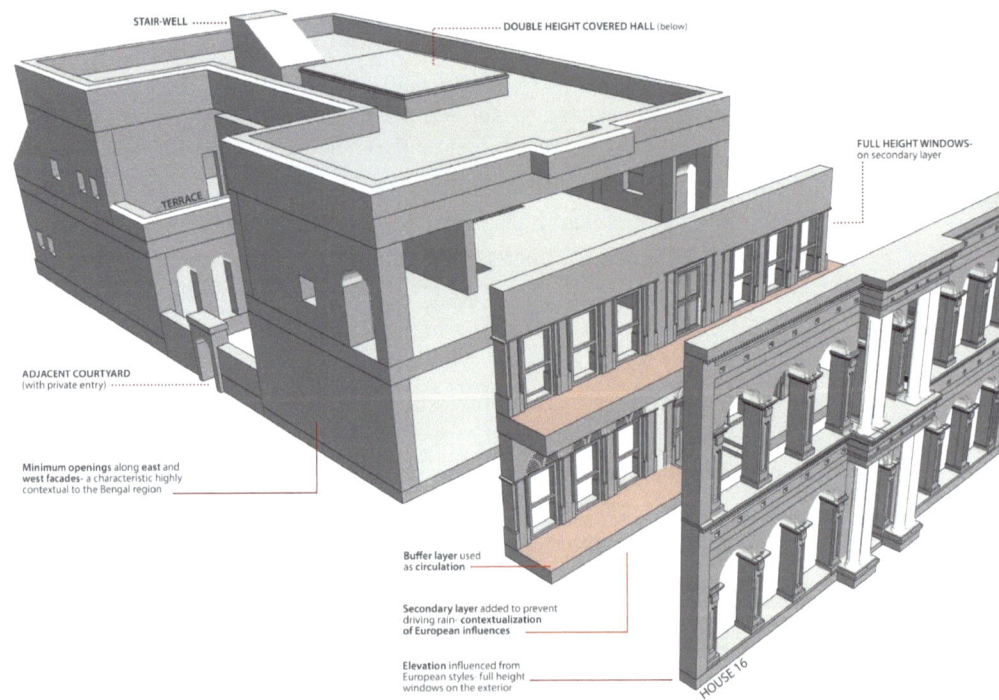

66 | RE-IMAGINING BENGAL

GROUND FLOOR PLAN

FIGURE 4.8: Plan of Houses 16-18-20-22 showing various zones and circulation
The symmetry in circulation was probably inspired by European influences of grand symmetrical arrangement as seen in Victorian/Renaissance residences or public buildings.

Source: Author

be deduced that the circulation elements toward the street side were used by male occupants and visitors, and the circulation elements at the rear were used by the women of the house.

It is also important to note here that House No. 18-20-22 (see Figure 4.7, 4.8 and 4.9) has a redundant presence of symmetry. Although the above explanation is possibly true for House No. 16, it appears that 18-20-22 have followed simply the physical influence of using European styles. House No. 16's two sets of stairs can be justified by the private/public segregation of use based on their size and scale, House No. 18-20-22's cannot be.

FIGURE 4.9: Interior of House 16
The hall shows European influence adapted to local context.

Source: Author

Rare presence of courtyard and hall
While the courtyard is a local typology, the hall is an adapted colonial feature. Here the courtyard is placed at the back of the building as opposed to centrally. It provides secondary access to House No. 16 from adjacent spaces (the use of these adjacent spaces is unknown). Some possible use of the courtyard with the boundary wall could have been to bring in light, to create a personalized garden / green space, to provide a private secondary entry. Comparatively the double height hall is a more conventional adaptation of colonial elements, possibly placed to entertain guests.

Access to water through personalized ghat
Generally, in rural/urban homesteads, *ghats* (informal boat docks) are used as public spaces. In Bengal, these spaces typically act as nodes of socialization for community members. They are generally placed centrally with several homesteads sharing them. The functions of these *ghats* can include bathing, washing, etc. However, in House No. 16, it is seen that the ghat is personalized, providing access, security

and privacy only to the members of a single family/house; showing affluence of the owners. The space that pressed the *ghat* is also separated physically by a low wall that supports this inference. The surrounding moat of Panam Nagar, the *Pankhiraj* Canal must have had limited users providing entry through water. It can be also inferred that Panam Nagar had controlled social interactions (possibly with apparent division in the society of wealth or financial strata).

European style windows adapted to maintain sub-continental approach
Windows in the homesteads of Bengal are usually at or above 3 feet level; mostly due to avoid driving rain, common during the monsoon season. However, at the houses in Panam Nagar (House 16 included) full height windows are seen arranged symmetrically to doors. This is essentially a European influence and does not reflect the local context. Consideration for the local context can be noted in the west and east surfaces of all houses, having minimum openings to avoid heat gain in buildings and maximum openings on the north and south surfaces to allow the best possible ventilation. This is highly contextual to Bengal. There are two layers of openings on the north and south having full height windows. This implies that the European elements (of full height windows) were adapted to suit the local context. The buffer space in between the second set of full height openings protects the internal spaces from driving rain.

HOUSE 38
Adapted zoning inspired from rural vernacular
The house (see Figure 4.10 & 4.11) has a rare semi-open porch that actually doesn't directly open to the street, rather has a buffer in the form of a front yard or garden. However, this layer is transparent and easily accessible. The house can be divided into few distinct zones: public zone with the garden, veranda and living rooms at south, semi-public zone with part of the corridor, a zone of transition where the corridor opens up to two staircases surrounding an open to sky courtyard, private zone with bedrooms and a service zone at the north.

While the rural courtyard serves both as an accumulator and service zone, social space and distributor to various spaces surrounding them; this role was directed and distributed to different parts in the compact linear form. This can be categorized under adapted spaces

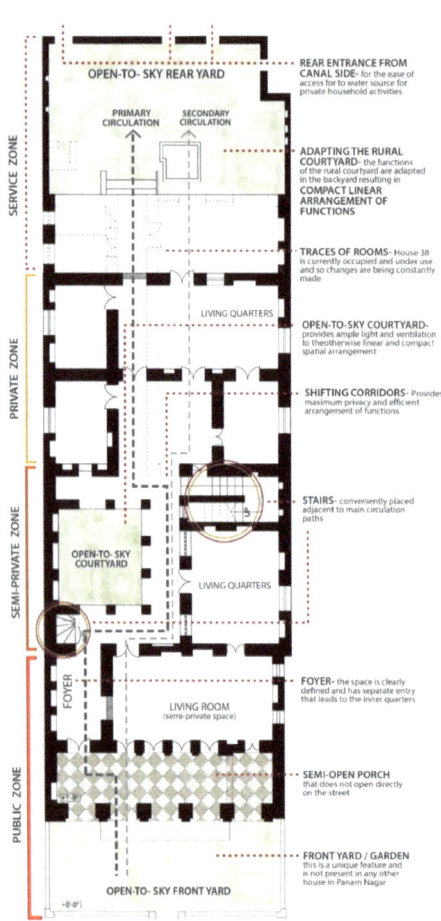

GROUND FLOOR PLAN

FIGURE 4.10: Plan of House 38 showing various zones and circulation
The house can be divided into few distinct zones: public zone with the garden, veranda and living rooms at south, semi-public zone with part of the corridor, a zone of transition where the corridor opens up to two staircases surrounding an open to sky courtyard, private zone with bedrooms and a service zone at north.

Source: Author

such as the zone of transition (which also provides a visual link to the upper level), service zone for kitchen and bath, etc., and the upper level terrace providing zone of recreation. The service is mostly hidden at the back of the house in north with minimum openings. The yard at the back provides ample space for kitchen and other service activities with privacy. It is curious to note that while these spaces were some of the early attempts of interpreting and adapting

FIGURE 4.11: Exterior of House 38
The house has a rare semi-open porch that actually doesn't directly open to the street, rather has a buffer in the form of a front yard or garden.

Source: Author

rural courtyards, they were equally successful in creating the natural ambience of these spaces.

The living room at ground floor faces the street, the spaces are layered here. The small garden adjacent to street and the semi-open veranda buffers the living room from street. These two spaces provide privacy for the living room activities visually while the space remains physically accessible. A separate in the west provides a private entry for the inner quarters.

Climate sensitive orientation and openings
The two storied house has a north-south orientation with the entrance at south. The house has mostly solid walls at east and west facades with few openings. The open to sky terrace and double height courtyard provides ample link with outdoor and compensates for the narrow north and south facades, bringing in light and air and also providing a visual link between floors. This configuration resembles traditional linear shophouses with multiple courtyards.

Flexible circulation
The house has a unique proper foyer space which provides a separate entry for household members. The linear corridor running through the plan from south to north provides major circulation at ground level. The corridor shifts and turns to provide maximum privacy for the inner quarters and bedrooms. The corridor opens up to an open to sky courtyard and an internal lounge. Both of them have an adjacent staircase. The double height courtyard provides a visual link between the two floors. From consideration of privacy, the narrow staircase adjacent to the double height courtyard has an indirect entrance at ground level, but opens up at the first floor in a common area. The main staircase at east provides a visual link with first floor activities where one gets a glimpse of the first floor through the open to sky courtyard. Visual link closely ties horizontal and vertical movements here.

The house's spatial and circulation pattern has a close resemblance to typical contemporary houses of Bangladesh. The layout shows an uncanny similarity in circulation, arrangement of living room, kitchen and bedrooms. Considering this aspect, the house can be considered an early example of how the urban houses would transform in the next one hundred years (from its construction) or so.

Zone of proximity with neighbors
The first floor terrace at north provides recreational space and also a platform for social interaction with neighbors. Proximity of forms (with narrow/no gap in between two houses) provides scope for visual and verbal interaction. However, this interaction is primarily intended for the inner quarters as the number of openings in east and west facade are sparse and narrow. Adjacent forms of the houses not only provide visual contact; it was also physical in cases with selected openings where two house share walls. This shows the existence of close social relationships and trust among neighbors.

CONCLUSION

The case studies attempt to shed light on the missing link in local housing typology and bring forth several important issues such as adapted housing forms reflecting socio-cultural values, social status and identity; meeting the spatial, socio-cultural and visual requirements. In most cases the adaptation is intelligent, rarely directly copying the source. Rather they show a curious flexibility where personal lifestyle choices and economic status played a vital role. Climate and culture always play an active role in the adaptation process starting with importing European elements, finding a balance with local elements and ultimately creating a strong hybrid style.

An important finding is the sensitive hierarchy of public to private spaces showing clever spatial territoriality. Selective use of space separators ensured privacy and made a more cohesive social living possible. In several cases the transformed spaces were the result of lifestyle changes or property subdivision. As every household had different behavior politics, it was reflected in space formation.

The case studies show how the built environment of Panam Nagar facilitated human engagement, experience and socialization. Within linear spaces they play with issues such as visibility, privacy, climatic requirements, movement, social interaction, etc. They show a process where architecture afforded the people to form, interpret and create spaces with imported elements adapted to local needs. Here physical spaces optimized human interactions and maintained intended social frameworks.

The houses offer multi-layered spaces to foster active, engaged relationships among users and neighbors, creating a sense of communal stewardship and lived connection. The inter-subjective spaces of Panam Nagar offer intersecting and dissecting personal and public–social trajectories and remind that as social beings the inner spaces and in-between shared spaces of these houses provide an arena for some of the best possibilities of community living. The spaces are often quite simple while being abstract and open to interpretation in others, giving a hint of some undisclosed plot shared by the society of that period. This mystery invites one to keep exploring these spaces.

REFERENCES

- Ahmed, B. (2014). *The Adaptive Re-Use of Painam Nagar*. (Bachelor of Architecture), BRAC University, Dhaka.

- Ahmed, G. (1993). *Sonargaon Parichiti* (in Bengali). In R. Karim & S. Asgar (Eds.), *Sonargaoer Itihas: utsho o upadaon* (pp. 303-313). Dhaka: Rahman Group of Industries.
- Ahmed, I. (2006). A participatory approach to conservation: Working with community to save the cultural heritage of Panamnagar. *BRAC University Journal*, III(2), 25-33.
- Ahmed, I. (2007). Panamnagar: a participatory approach of conservation to save the cultural heritage. Paper presented at *the 18th CAA Conference on Society, Architects and Emerging issues*, Dhaka.
- Ahmed, N. (1984). *Discover the Monuments of Bangladesh - A Guide to Their History, Location and Development*. Dhaka: The University Press Limited (UPL)
- Ahmed, N. (1986). *Buildings of the British Raj in Bangladesh* (J. Sanday Ed.). Dhaka: The University Press Limited (UPL)
- Ali, T. (2007, 16 April). Panamnagar Unscientific restoration defacing heritage. *The Daily Star*. Retrieved from www.thedailystar.net/2007/04/26/d7042601107.htm
- Ali, Z. F. (1990). Painam Nagar, Sonargaon. In A. H. Imamuddin & K. R. Longeteig (Eds.), *Architectural and Urban Conservation in the Islamic World* (Vol. I, pp. 147-163). Geneva: The Aga Khan Trust for Culture.
- The Antiquities Act Act No. XIV of 1968 (amended 22 September 1976) Stat. (1968).
- Brown, P. (1956). *Indian Architecture (Islamic Period)*. Bombay D.B. Taraporevala Sons & Co.
- Evarts, H. (2007). World monuments fund announces 2008 world monuments watch list of 100 most endangered sites. Retrieved 3 October, 2016, from https://www.wmf.org/sites/default/files/press_releases/pdfs/2008%20Watch%20List.pdf
- Grover, S. (1981). *The architecture of India, Islamic (727-1707 AD)*. New Delhi Vikas Publishing House.
- Hussain, A. B. M. (1997). *Sonargaon Panam*. Dhaka: Asiatic Society of Bangladesh.
- Hussain, A. B. M. (2007). *Cultural Survey of Bangladesh Series: Architecture*. Dhaka: Asiatic Society of Bangladesh.
- Kaderi, S. B. H. (1998). *Oitijjher Sonargaon* (In Bengali). Dhaka Tajmahal Machine Press.
- Khan, M. H. (2014, 5 May). Panam. Retrieved 3 October 2016, from http://en.banglapedia.org/index.php?title=Panam
- Khatun, H. (2006). *Iqlim Sonargaon - history, jurisdiction, monuments*. Dhaka: Academic Press and Publisher.
- Mowla, Q. A., & Reza, M. (2000). Stylistic Evolution of Architecture in Bangladesh. *Journal of the Asiatic Society of Bangladesh*, 45(1), 31-58.

- Panamnagar declared archeological site. (2003, March 23). *The Daily New Age*.
- Roy, S. (1891). *Subornogramer itihas* (in Bengali). Calcutta. : Dey's Publishing.
- Sarkar, S. J. (Ed.). (1948). *History of Bengal Volume II*. Delhi B.R. PUblishing Corporation.
- Shaikh, Z. U., & Rahman, M. (2009). Twenty five buildings - frozen museum of Panam Nagar. In M. Rahman (Ed.), *Old but new new but old* (pp. 280-323). Dhaka: UNESCO
- Taylor, J. (1840). *A Sketch of the Topography & Statistics of Dacca*: G.H. Huttmann, Military Orphan Press.
- Wise, J. (1874). Notes on Sonargaon, Eastern Bengal. *Journal of the Asiatic Society of Bengal* (XLIII), 82-92.
-

FIGURE 5.1: Verandah of Pogose school
Nineteenth century detailing of wooden and iron beams, window shades and door louvers in Pogose school.

Source: Author

SOCIAL CAPITAL IN PARTICIPATORY INFORMAL HERITAGE MANAGEMENT: CASES FROM OLD DHAKA

Iftekhar Ahmed

HERITAGE IN TRADITIONAL URBAN SETTLEMENTS: SOME REFLECTIONS

Heritage provides a sense of attachment and point of reference of who we are. Heritage may be seen as a cultural continuity inherited in time. David Lowenthal observes, "Only by studying the lives of past people and by learning what had happened in history could people understand their present selves and circumstances and hope to foresee what life would be like in times to come... hence the past was a fount of useful lessons, lessons that could serve as precept for the present and the future" (Lowenthal, 1993). In the socio-cultural milieu of most traditional urban settlements, heritage holds a very special place. Heritage in traditional urban settlements offers extraordinary cultural richness, especially so when they are rooted in places of *living* communities. Bonnici observes, "Cultural heritage refers to goods which have been 'inherited' and have a public value, and that therefore need to be preserved for future generations, to be in turn inherited by them" (Bonnici, 2005). Heritage provides identity and a link to past for local communities. Hewison observes, "heritage represents some kind of security, a point of reference, a refuge, perhaps, something visible and tangible which...seems stable and unchanged" (Bagguley, Mark-Lawson, & Shapiro, 1990). Winter and Daly shares a similar view, "Heritage may be seen as a cultural continuity inherited in time. It gives us a sense of attachment and point of reference of who we are. Heritage typically centers on the notion of culture-natures that are inherited from those that came before us and are safeguarded in the present in order to be bestowed for the benefit of future generations" (Winter & Daly, 2012).

The Faro Convention (Europe, 2005) in Article 2 seeks to define cultural heritage as: "a group of resources inherited from the past which people identify, independently of ownership, as a reflection and expression of their constantly evolving values, beliefs, knowledge and traditions. It includes all aspects of the environment resulting from the interaction between people and places through time". The Convention then defines a heritage community: "a heritage community consists of people who value specific aspects of cultural heritage which they wish, within the framework of public action, to sustain and transmit to future generations". The Faro Convention (Europe, 2005) also declares in Article 4: "a. everyone, alone or collectively, has the right to benefit from the cultural heritage and to contribute towards its enrichment; b. everyone, alone or collectively, has the responsibility to respect the cultural heritage of others as much as their own heritage".

Where communities are directly involved (Cnaan & Milofsky, 2007) and heritage are living, by their very nature, the heritage never remain fixed and static. The urban environment changes rapidly, especially so since the second half of twentieth century. Amidst this frenzy of urban development, communities and their attachment to local heritage have often been ignored in many conservation efforts (Mui, 2008), especially in high density cities; ultimately making the heritage *soulless*. Heritage is precious, once lost it cannot be recreated. "By dealing with built heritage we must be aware that this is a non-renewable source" (Kilian, 2008). A key issue in heritage conservation, especially where place and people are an active part of heritage, is to interpret and define heritage through local experiences. Thus, it is critical to understand how the communities of the traditional neighborhoods continue to safeguard and manage local heritage with their common wisdom and knowledge. This can potentially benefit in sustaining the heritage for future. Rather than approaching heritage conservation or future development in the conventional way, often governed by the well-known Eurocentric heritage conservation charters, it may be beneficial to examine the way the communities in traditional urban settlements retain their cultural continuity in a fast changing urban environment around them. This chapter examines these critical issues through the findings of an empirical field study in the traditional neighborhoods of Old Dhaka.

MAHALLAS OF OLD DHAKA: PLACE, PEOPLE AND MEANING OF HERITAGE

Dhaka, the capital of Bangladesh, is a mega city of 15.4 million people (WPR, 2016) with the greater urban area encompassing

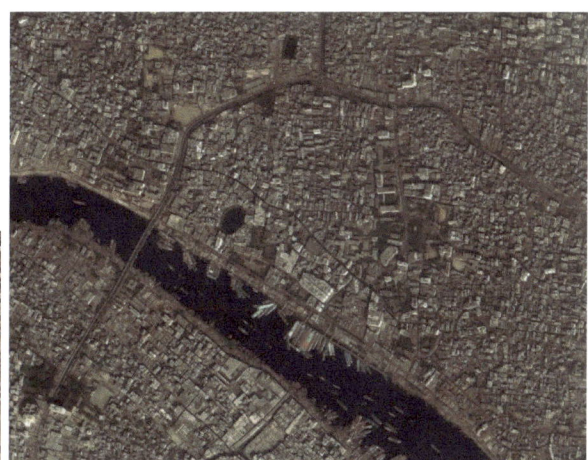

FIGURE 5.2: Aerial views of Old Dhaka showing high density traditional neighborhoods
Unplanned organic growth of Old Dhaka. The indigenous urban units are several high density traditional neighborhoods locally known as mahalla.

Source: Author and Digital Globe, 2017

approximately 1,530 square km (IMF, 2013). The city has a recorded history of about 400 years (established as a Mughal province in 1608). However, archaeological evidence suggest the city actually existed several centuries before this. Most of the city's rich architectural heritage lie in the historic core primarily developed on the bank of river *Buriganga* (see Figure 5.2) for trade and transportation. This older part of the city is locally known as Old Dhaka. There was no plan for Old Dhaka, the physical formation shows organic growth. The indigenous urban units are several traditional neighborhoods locally known as *mahalla*. There are several traditional *mahallas* in Old Dhaka with close-knit communities that date back two to three centuries.

Taylor and Singleton define community in terms of the following characteristics: (a) relations have a certain stability, i.e. those in the community interact with some degree of regularity, (b) members interact on several fronts, (c) relations are unmediated by the state, and (d) members have shared beliefs and preferences which go beyond the particular collective action problem (Taylor & Singleton, 1993). The traditional communities in the *mahallas* of Old Dhaka satisfy all the criterion. The people of Old Dhaka are different from the modern parts of the city, with their long legacy, unique culture, lifestyle, language and mannerism. All these combine to create an unique yet indefinable aura very specific to the area.

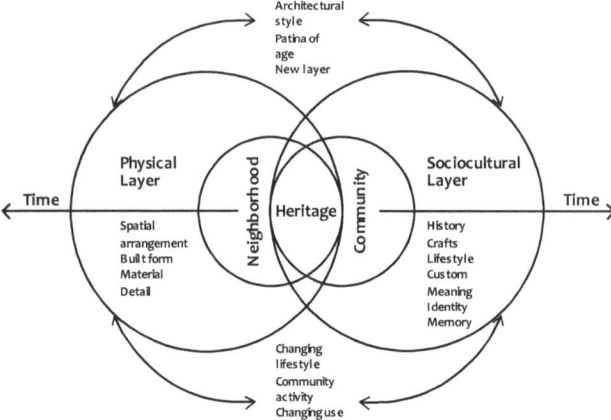

FIGURE 5.3: Continuity of *mahallas* showing growth of physical and sociocultural layers

In mahallas of Old Dhaka, the physical and sociocultural layers are palimpsests of several elements essential for community living. Each layer, physical or sociocultural, gets enhanced with time.

Source: Author

Each of the *mahallas* are traditional enclaves with unique character shaped over several centuries where the social and physical formation of rural communities was successfully adapted in the early urban settlements. Often formed by association of a key craft, trade or religion, the *mahallas* originated as the living quarters of specialized artisans or traders, as clearly evident in their names, such as *Shankharibazar* (market of *Shankha* makers), *Kosaituli* (neighborhood of butchers), *Tantibazar* (market of weavers), etc. While few of the *mahallas* couldn't survive the changing socioeconomic and political circumstances, others continue till today with the original communities.

The *mahallas* are often very compact, deceptively narrow at first glance, while bustling with energy and activity in the inner layer with street front shops and bazaars. They have a great social system with close-knit community living and co-existence; rare in other parts of the city. With time, these *mahallas* became richer both in physical and sociocultural elements that form and sustain them. The physical and sociocultural layers (see Figure 5.3) are palimpsests of several elements essential for community living. Each layer, physical or sociocultural, gets enhanced with time. A physical element such as construction technique or spatial arrangements gets enriched with age, while the local customs, practices and meaning gradually evolve with need of changing time.

FIGURE 5.4: Tangible and intangible heritage elements of Old Dhaka
Tangible heritage includes a wide range of religious, civic and private buildings, unique organic spatial layout, hybrid architectural styles, local materials and crafts, rich details and ornamentations. Whereas intangible range from clay pottery and idol making, vernacular construction techniques such as Chini-tikri, traditional crafts such as Shankha and terracotta, legacy of traditional foods such as Baker-khani, etc.

Source: Author

As meaning evolves with time, it is important to understand what heritage means to local communities of Old Dhaka. The meaning of local heritage has taken shape over the years as a combination of individual and collective experiences, memories, shared values and everyday lifestyle in the communities. The meaning in cases becomes the identity of that particular *mahalla* where the locals and visitors distinguish the locality through heritage. The heritage makes them stand out among other *mahallas*. UNESCO observes, "Any city's future must be anchored in its individual identity. Its 'urban heritage' must be the starting point for the development of urban policy. This heritage and its accumulation – the history of a city, its neighborhoods and its residents – must be studied, recorded and told" (UNESCO, 1996). Where people share a collective memory, often complex and intertwined; it strengthens the social bond in communities. Memory association is an important part of heritage (tangible and intangible) and its attachment to a particular place. Heritage becomes a carrier of memory and ensures cultural continuity; the process is an integral part of everyday life in the traditional *mahallas*.

The tangible heritage in traditional *mahallas* of Old Dhaka includes a wide range of religious, civic and private building, unique organic spatial layout, hybrid architectural styles, local materials and crafts, rich details and ornamentations (see Figure 5.4). In Old Dhaka, heritage is layered and hybrid; showing stylistic influences of traditional vernacular, Sultanate, Mughal and British colonial period in local architecture, urban form, texture and morphology, gradually accumulated over the years (Dani, 1956; Imamuddin, 1982). With age and inevitable process of urban change, often new parts are added and/or original layers are altered in tangible heritage. Comparatively, intangible heritage elements have remained more or less intact or even got enriched with time. In Old Dhaka, intangible heritage breathe life into tangible heritage, they impart and nurture their value.

Intangible heritage elements of Old Dhaka are varied and rich, ranging from clay pottery and idol making, vernacular construction techniques such as *Chini-tikri*, traditional crafts such as *Shankha* and terracotta, legacy of traditional foods such as *Baker-khani*, etc. (see Figure 5.4). These elements develop on the canvas of local lifestyles, history, oral stories, collective memory, rituals, customs, festivals, meanings, identity, etc. Intangible heritage elements are unquantifiable, abstract in nature; they are the spiritual assets of local communities. Survival and growth of intangible heritage, depends on two factors: how actively heritage buildings are being used and whether local communities have strong social structures.

From their inception, the *mahallas* existed because the community members shared a strong social bond. In special cases, where the root is religious, the community becomes almost sacred, surrounded by several religious forms and symbols. The sense of community and social living are not only essential for survival but also highly cherished. One can feel the presence of a proud social bond in frequent use of the first person plural 'we', 'ours' (*amra* and *amader* in Bengali) in everyday speech. This helped them to cope with shortage of urban amenities in recent times. This shortage is often dire but still the communities continue to live in the *mahallas*. Field study reveals that they value the psychological comfort that living in the community of their ancestors provide them above the physical facilities. While in other parts of the city social network get weaker every day, the bond between community members are remarkably deep and rooted in place in Old Dhaka. This is reflected in everyday communal life, social activities, tastes, liking, abilities, limitations, and above all, the lifestyle of the communities. Over several generations, these have helped to create a strong base of social capital in the *mahallas* of Old Dhaka.

COMMUNITY AND SOCIAL CAPITAL IN OLD DHAKA

In an attempt to criticize neoclassical economic theory for its narrowly individualistic and atomistic understanding of human capital, Loury introduced the idea of social capital in 1977:

> *The social context within which individual maturation occurs strongly conditions what otherwise equally competent individuals can achieve. This implies that absolute equality of opportunity, where an individual's chance to succeed depends only on his or her innate capabilities, is an ideal that cannot be achieved.... An individual's social origin has an obvious and important effect on the amount of resources that is ultimately invested in his or her development. It may thus be useful to employ a concept of "social capital" to represent the consequences of social position in facilitating acquisition of the standard human capital characteristics (Loury, 1977).*

French sociologist Pierre Bourdieu (Bourdieu, 1985), concurred with the idea and argued that social capital is a set of power relations that constitute a variety of realms and social interactions normally thought of as noneconomic. He observed that social networks should not simply be equated to the products of those social relationships, for doing so would render invisible social networks that might be very dense but nonetheless unable to generate resources because of lack of access. According to him, relationships of mutual acquaintance and recognition or in other words, to membership in a group which provides each of its members with the backing of the collectivity owned capital.

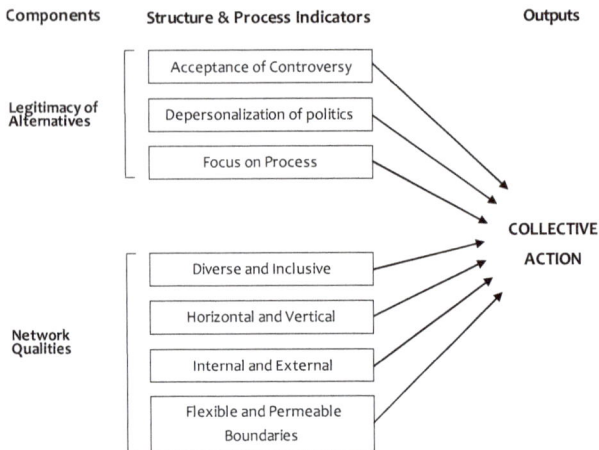

FIGURE 5.5: The entrepreneurial social infrastructure model
Social capital is realized by individuals, it is not embodied in any particular person, but rather is embedded in people's social relationships. The diagram elaborates this argument to various components, structure and process indicators.

Source: Author, based on Flora & Flora (Flora & Flora, 1993)

Following Loury and Bourdieu, James Coleman brought the idea of social capital into mainstream social sciences and defined, "It is not a single entity, but a variety of different entities having two characteristics in common: They all consist of some aspect of social structure, and they facilitate certain actions of individuals who are within the structure... a given form of social capital that is valuable in facilitating certain actions may be useless or even harmful for others. Unlike other forms of capital, social capital inheres in the structure of relations between actors and among actors". He then argued, "social capital arises or disappears without anyone's willing it into or out of being and is thus even less recognized and taken account of in social action than its already intangible character would warrant" (Coleman, 1988). Loury (1977), Bourdieu (1985), and Coleman (1988) commonly argued that even though social capital is realized by individuals, it is not embodied in any particular person, but rather is embedded in people's social relationships. This argument was further elaborated to various components, structure and process indicators by Flora and Flora (1993) as shown in Figure 5.5. Here, the authors divide the major components such as legitimacy of alternatives and network qualities (of social relations) into several smaller indicators that give a clear expression of how social infrastructure helps to generate social capital.

Social capital is a valuable asset in the traditional communities that have been continuing for hundreds of years. Without social capital communities fail to survive, as evident in many contemporary neighborhoods (Dolff-Bonekämper, 2009). In traditional enclaves, people value the bond that exists in communities and relationship with neighbors more than their physical environment (Council of Europe, 2005). The *mahallas* Old Dhaka are rich in social capital accumulated over several generations spanning few centuries in cases. The origin of the social capital is close social network; the glue that holds the communities together. The mahallas with stronger social network have retained the original community, the origin being people living in close social contact, trusting each other and depending on each other in socioeconomic matters of everyday life. Several components generate social capital in Old Dhaka: greater social trust among the community members, social, religious and cultural norms, vernacular knowledge of crafts, traditional construction styles, informal community bodies, and more importantly, social network, infrastructure, routine and special collective actions taken by the community.

Putnam expanded the idea of social capital after Loury (1977), Bourdieu (1985), and Coleman (1988) in terms of how social groups actually use social capital: first, social capital is transformed from something realized by individuals to something possessed (or not possessed) by either individuals or groups of people in regions, communities, cities, countries, or continents. Second, it is conflated with civil society, or more accurately, with a particular neo-Tocquevillean view of civil society. Thus, voluntary, non-government associations, based on trust, become the institutions through which social capital is generated (Putnam, 1993). On a similar note, Portes and Sensenbrenner reason, "Social capital is generated by individual members' disciplined compliance with group expectations. However, the motivating force in this case is not value convictions, but the anticipation of utilities associated with 'good standing' in a particular collectivity" (Portes & Sensenbrenner, 1993).

The major theorists of social capital agree that it is generally common for social networks to lead to generation of social capital through exercise of collective group activities. In a later study, Loury defined social capital as, "naturally occurring social relationships among persons which promote or assist the acquisition of skills and traits valued in the marketplace . . . an asset which may be as significant as financial bequests in accounting for the maintenance of inequality in our society" (Loury, 1992). This skill set is the origin of social capital in Old Dhaka as most of the *mahallas* developed as enclaves of specialist craftsmen or traders where the communities originated from people's ability to work together for shared purposes. Fukuyama relates this in his definition of social capital as: "the ability of people to work together for common purposes in groups and organizations" (Fukuyama, 1995). From their inception, the communities of Old Dhaka had the platform for people to work together and had a strong base of social capital. From this, few communities led social organizations were developed. These informal community bodies in the *mahallas* of Old Dhaka facilitated people's shared social activities.

COMMUNITY BODIES OF OLD DHAKA: LOCAL VOICES AND ACTIONS

During the British colonial rule of about two hundred years, Dhaka was a provincial capital, much lesser in significance than Kolkata (then Calcutta). Even though the British had a provincial government here, in effect it was not quite adequate to look after the everyday problems of communities of Old Dhaka. This was perhaps the incentive for development of community bodies of Old Dhaka. Even though their existence can be traced back before this, it is during the colonial rule that they flourished. The community led social bodies often worked with site-specific social orders (such as the *Shankharis* (*Shankha* makers) living in *Shankharibazar*, Tantis (weavers) living in *Tantibazar*, etc.). In the *mahallas*, community members decided to be together in a close social environment for safety and socioeconomic and cultural benefits. Originating as the living quarters of specialized groups of people, every community had their unique set of requirements. This need gave rise to the formation of informal community bodies (such as the *Panchayet*) to take care of local community interests, to resolve conflicts with adjacent neighborhoods and take other common community led social actions. Starting with simpler everyday matters, their responsibility gradually extended to deciding common social, economic and cultural issues of the *mahallas*.

Among the various surviving informal community bodies of Old Dhaka, the oldest is the *Panchayet*. Several *mahallas* of Old Dhaka still has a functioning *Panchayet*, e.g. Kosaituli. *Panchayet* literally means 'body of five', signifying the initial number of members such bodies had. James Taylor described the existence of *Panchayets* of Old Dhaka and how they worked in 1840 (Taylor, 1840). James Wise, an eminent British historian, gave one of the early statements on *Panchayet* in 1883, "The *Panchayet* intended to serve the common people and bring forth their well-being" (Wise, 1883). A more comprehensive account of the Panchayet system can be found in Khwaja Azams work in 1907 where he stated neither the Muslim rulers nor the Mughals had introduced this and most probably the system existed even before that (Azam, 1907).

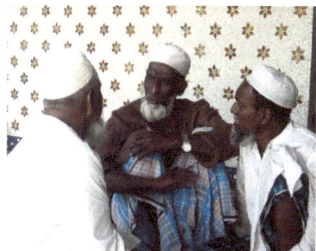

FIGURE 5.6: Panchayet house and activities in Old Dhaka
Panchayets were formed to take care of trade or professional interests very similar to professional guilds.

Source: Author

Discussion with the elders of the *mahallas* revealed that during the British rule, along with the greater Mahalla Panchayets (see Figure 5.6), different groups or castes (in case of the Hindus) had their own *Panchayet* lower in the hierarchy than the *Mahalla Panchayets*. They were formed to take care of the trade or professional interests (for example *Panchayets* for specialized craftsmen *Shankharis*), very similar to professional guilds. Oral history suggests that these smaller *Panchayets* may have preceded the *Mahalla Panchayets* to serve entire communities.

Even though the organization varies among the *mahallas*, the contemporary structure of Panchayets consists of a Shabhapati or President, Vice-president, treasurer, secretary and general members of various numbers, with all the members having equal voting right.

They are generally most respected members of communities, and government representatives such as ward commissioners do not have the spontaneous respect they command from community members. Primarily having sociopolitical responsibilities, they manage everyday social issues in the *mahallas*, act for the common good of the communities and are democratic and secular in decision making. For example, every year the *Panchayet Shabhapati* of *Shankharibazar* takes important decisions on the organization and management of the major Puja (e.g. *Lakshmi* and *Swarashwati Puja*) celebrations.

Parallel to managing social matters, Mahalla Panchayets collectively handle physical issues in the neighborhood; an important part of Panchayet's responsibilities is the management of the local heritage structures. The mechanisms of heritage management are informal in nature, but has proven highly effective in Old Dhaka. This is evident as the local heritage has survived in good shape for hundreds of years. To appreciate the cases of informal heritage management and the role social capital plays in them, it is important to have an insight into the formal system of heritage conservation in Dhaka.

FORMAL HERITAGE CONSERVATION IN DHAKA: CONSTRAINTS OF THE PROCESS

The Department of Archaeology under the Ministry of Cultural Affairs of Bangladesh is the governing body for conservation and management of heritage buildings and sites. Interview with major officials of the Department reveals that even though there are positions of archaeologists, very few have proper training for the post. There are no conservation experts in the Department. Most of the conservation projects are supervised by diploma engineers with basic knowledge of civil engineering with little or no idea about conservation process or architectural styles. Due to lack of research personnel, no real research is done prior to undertaking conservation projects. Naturally, this results in poor quality restoration that further damages the heritage in most cases. Even the number of engineers is inadequate with fourteen working now and the Department's requirement being at least thirty. This puts greater burden on them where one engineer has to look after four to five conservation projects simultaneously, having even lesser time to spare.

The heritage of Dhaka is diverse; ranging from community *owned* buildings (such as mosques that are used every day) to state owned monuments with restricted entry. To manage and protect the vast range of heritage, the legislations have to be dynamic and up-to-date. Unfortunately, the scenario is completely reverse. Currently, the Antiquities Act of 1968 is used as the governing legislation for protection of local heritage (The Antiquities Act, 1968). 'Antiquity' is defined in the act as, "any ancient product of human activity, movable of immovable, illustrative of art, architecture, craft, custom, literature, morals, politics, religion, warfare, science or of any aspect of civilization or culture, any ancient object or site of historical, ethnographical, anthropological, military or scientific interest, and any other ancient object or class of such objects declared by the Central Government, by notification in the official Gazette, to be an antiquity for the purposes of this Act." (The Antiquities Act, 1968): article 2, section c). The Department of Archaeology follows this definition and lists a heritage for protection only when it is at least one hundred years old, interpreting the term 'ancient' with a time frame (of 100 years). The current list of protected heritage includes three hundred and ninety-seven buildings and seven sites. Several important and vulnerable heritage (which are less than hundred years old) wither and decay as they couldn't make the list.

Conservation is very low on priority while government allots funds. The Department of Archaeology only receives about 30 to 40 thousand US dollars yearly to conserve and manage the listed heritage. Fund allotted to selected buildings needs to be prioritized. In very special cases, a vulnerable heritage building/site (in urgent need for conservation) gets funded with a time frame. When this expires, the fund is called back. This has led to several hurried restoration projects with little or no research, executing the work without any expert supervision, actually damaging the heritage than protecting them. A recent example is Panam Nagar, a linear heritage township of forty-nine abandoned street-front houses, dating back to late nineteenth century. Being abandoned in the 1960s (as the owners fled to India facing post-partition riots), illegally occupied from 1970s until 2004 (with no maintenance), the heritage township became highly vulnerable.

Panam Nagar was declared a protected archaeological site in March, 2003 and subsequently evacuated in 2004. In 2005–2006 fiscal year, the government allotted a special fund of about 700 thousand USD for the first phase of conservation of Panam Nagar; to be spent within June 2007 (Ali, 2007). The Department of Archaeology was in a hurry to spend the fund and completed the project within time. Restoration work started in sixteen buildings without proper research or documentation. Several experts commented that the Department didn't involve any historian, archaeologist or architect in the restoration; rather hired masons supervised by diploma engineers to carry out the job. A site official even commented that "masons know how to do the job" (Ali, 2007). As a result, the sixteen buildings were partially or fully distorted or defaced.

Due to lack of knowledge, the supervising diploma engineers of the Department and common masons used flat and plain thick plaster in the improper restoration work. It partially/fully replaced original stucco ornamentations, meticulously proportioned molded curves, decorated cornices, lintels and pilasters of hybrid style, inspired by British colonial and Mughal architecture. Delicately detailed and ornamented friezes, pilaster, cornices and colonnades were insensitively replaced with out of proportion, odd and alien features. The original construction used plaster of conch shell powder with a smooth finish mimicking white marble. This was replaced with an ordinary coating of lime and *surki* (brick grains) of a different color (see Figure 5.7).

Local conservation expert Dr. Abu Syed Ahmed, who was also a member of the advisory committee on the project, stated:

FIGURE 5.7: Improper restoration work at Panam Nagar, left: before and right: after

Due to lack of knowledge, the supervising diploma engineers and common masons used flat and plain thick plaster that partially/fully replaced original stucco ornamentations, meticulously proportioned molded curves, decorated cornices, lintels and pilasters of hybrid style, inspired by British colonial and Mughal architecture.

Source: Author

"Conservation work of such a historical site must involve conservation architects, general historians, geographers, archaeologists and historians of art and heritage... the government agency is actually destroying the fundamental heritage features of the site in the name of restoration, engaging mere masons and construction contractors in the job. The DoA is not going by the recommendations of the advisory committee, instead they have bypassed the committee" (Ali, 2007). The unplanned restoration project partially destroyed uniqueness and authenticity of the heritage township and did more damage than the illegal occupants in the last five decades. When the civil society noticed that the restoration work was rather insensitive to the original style, unskilled and damaged the buildings rather than protecting them, there was huge protesting to stop the work. Ultimately, the conservation project was suspended until further notice.

The case of Panam Nagar illustrates the key problems of formal heritage conservation in Dhaka. While on one hand, many important heritage buildings/sites don't make it to the list of protected heritage, and illegal alterations, modifications and even demolitions go unnoticed. On the other, the ones that do, often face the fate of Panam Nagar as the projects are undertaken without proper research, documenting or monitoring and executed by personnel without proper knowledge of conservation process; resulting in loss of authenticity and damage of entire historic fabrics in cases.

Another problem is the formal authority's failure to consider community attachment with heritage. As a result, the projects that are moderately conserved often become detached from the local communities and turns soulless. Within this context, this study explores the participatory informal heritage management system in Old Dhaka with selected case studies.

INFORMAL HERITAGE MANAGEMENT IN OLD DHAKA: TWO CASES

Dhaka, a megacity, has been facing exponential population growth during the past four decades. Roy and Sarkar observes: "Although urbanization is often associated with increasing national production and high per capita GDP, poverty remains a persistent feature of the urban life, both in terms of income and living conditions" (Roy & Sarker, 2006). Mainly due to ineffective political decisions, the economic growth has lagged far behind. The current yearly per capita income of Bangladesh is $1,180 (per capita income now $1,180, 2014). Old Dhaka is a highly built up area with greater than average population density compared to other parts of the city; thus generally

Key forces	Mechanism
Local representation	To make a common cause work, actively soliciting ideas and building support of stakeholders
Vernacular knowledge	To protect heritage buildings having *lost construction styles*, the critical factor is vernacular knowledge of local construction and material
Social capital	Communities with greater social capital have better solutions to problems compared to others
Common belongingness	Common consent leads to compliance and better implementation, a sense grows that 'this is ours'
Multiple ideas serve better	Where the idea of a few may fall short, ideas of many (who are knowledgeable) are generally successful

TABLE 5.1: Key forces and mechanism of informal heritage management process

Source: Author

more affected by the poor economic condition. No doubt, this makes managing community-based heritage more challenging.

While few of the communities are in relatively better economic condition; presence of greater social capital actually facilitates heritage management in the *mahallas*. Woolcock suggests that for social capital to be a useful concept at the micro (sub-societal) level, it must consist of two main dimensions: integration (intra-community ties) and linkage (extra-community networks) (Woolcock, 1998). In the *mahallas*, social capital increases in relation to community infrastructures and networks as well as existing social activities such as heritage management. Even though social capital is a pivotal force, there are other key forces at work that make informal heritage management possible in Old Dhaka, as shown in Table 5.1.

Dolff-bonekämper observes: "Exercise of the right to a heritage involves a right of access to a building site, the right to interpret and to take action, alone or with others, in a joint process of building heritage" (Dolff-bonekämper 2009). The social network in most of the traditional *mahallas* of Old Dhaka date back centuries. This legacy has helped to manage and maintain local heritage. The existence of community bodies such as *Panchayets* facilitates the informal heritage management process. As no external stakeholder is involved and community members are familiar with the heritage, decision making is generally informal, fast and effective. Even though the regular members of the community bodies take decisions, the majority of the local population is included in the process. The community bodies have a natural ability to engage communities in an active participatory process. Community bodies involve deliberation of multiple stakeholders from the community in the activities of informal heritage management. Most decisions are taken in consultation with the community body, building management committee (such as the Mosque committee) and in special cases with the advice of senior craftsmen.

Along with *Panchayets*, religious committees such as mosque or temple committees take a greater part of responsibilities in managing religious heritage structures such a mosque, temples, etc. *Panchayets* play a bigger role in managing secular heritage buildings such as schools. The types of heritage buildings include mosques, temples, church, school, etc. Informal heritage management process requires routine and emergency measures at various stages involving decision making, managing different actions among the community members and hired craftsmen and finally implementing as Table 5.2 shows.

Actions	Activities
Routine	Routine improvement and repair work, restoring façade and ornamentations
	Controlling improper modification, addition, alteration and demolition
	Repairing and maintaining shared streetscape and public space to maintain activities of community heritage buildings
	Adding appropriate new facilities in heritage buildings
Emergency	Treating structural problems in older buildings by adding reinforcement in vulnerable slabs and walls and treating damaged facades
	Using horizontal wooden and concrete beams to treat vertical cracks in walls

TABLE 5.2: Actions and activities of informal heritage management process

Source: Author

The issues of informal heritage management discussed can be best demonstrated with case studies where the process was successfully implemented. Two case studies of informal heritage management by community bodies are presented here to illustrate the key aspects of community-based heritage management process.

FIGURE 5.8: *Chini-tikri* work at Kosaituli mosque
The Kosaituli mosque is one the best surviving examples of colonial mosque architecture and displays a great variety of Chini-tikri work of finest quality. Chini-tikri work consists of intricate floral and geometric pattern of inlayed white and colored broken porcelain pieces.

Source: Author

KOSAITULI MOSQUE

Kosaituli Mosque, constructed in 1919 during the British colonial period, is one of the most ornate heritage mosques of Old Dhaka. The mosque is noted for some of the most striking *Chini-tikri* ornamentation; an intricate surface ornamentation done with broken porcelain pieces (see Figure 5.8). The mosque is managed by the mosque committee with support from the local Panchayet. As per the Antiquities Act of 1968, the Department of Archaeology only considers heritages that are 100 years old (i.e. ancient) to be included in the list of protected heritage. Kosaituli mosque is not 100 years old yet, so it went 'under the radar' (even though it is an important heritage) and was not included in the list; and is still *owned* by the community. As Old Dhaka's tradition, Kosaituli mosque is actively used by the local Muslim community for social purposes along with its main religious use. Sitting at the heart of the *mahalla*, the mosque is a living heritage and one of the main social gathering places of the local Muslim community.

The mosque is one the best surviving examples of colonial mosque architecture and displays a great variety of *Chini-tikri* work of finest quality. *Chini-tikri* work consists of intricate floral and geometric pattern of inlaid white and colored broken porcelain pieces. The craft originated as stone was not available in this region and it was a good replacement. *Chini-tikri* ornamentation requires lesser maintenance than other surface finishes. However, it is delicate, time consuming and expensive. CIF scientific working program 2005–2008 (Kilian, 2008) finds, "The fundamental role of crafts is to use materials in the best way in order to fulfill requirements in construction of buildings. It depends on capacity of the craftsman to offer the best and help to his client to find an economically acceptable solution. In the palaces of socioeconomic disparities… good practices show that traditional techniques and materials available on site are a possible solution. Preservation of existing skills, their social rediscovery and adaptation to new conditions is necessary in this field".

Even though there have been periodical maintenances, near the end of the twentieth century, the mosque's surface, especially the interior became vulnerable. As the mosque is regularly used for five daily prayers, the issue was detected and the mosque committee deliberated with local community members and Panchayet about possible actions. From the meetings two key challenges were identified: collecting funds and finding specialist craftsmen. The fund required was far greater than regular fund collected for managing the mosque. During the holy month of Ramadan, a special initiative was taken to collect funds for the restoration work and community members were urged to donate generously. The collection was possible due to presence of greater social capital in the community as there were generous donations from local shop owners as well as individuals.

Most of the original craftsmen specializing in *Chini-tikri* work came from Pakistan. The craftsmen working now are probably their third generation descendants who learned the craft through a system of apprenticeship. Due to the limited number of *Chini-tikri* work available, the number of craftsmen is ever diminishing with many shifting to other professions for survival. One of the few remaining senior master craftsmen of *Chini-tikri* was available. He was hired and supervised and executed the work with the support of a few new apprentices.

After solving issues of funding and craftsman, restoration of *chini-tikri* work started in 2004 and was completed in about two years. Even after generous donations, fund was still limited to complete the entire work in one go. Restoration was phased on a need basis. The mosque interior was vulnerable and required more immediate attention, it was restored first (during 2004–2005). The work cost about was 17 *lac* taka (approximately US$ 25,000). In the next phase, the exterior will be restored after the fund is collected. The mosque committee estimates it will cost about 30 lac taka (approximately US$ 43,000). A key aspect of the work was voluntary support (physical and social) from the community members during the entire two years. The entire restoration work was managed with supervision of the Mosque committee and support of local *Panchayet*. The detailing matched the original and the mosque interior fully regained its former glory.

Even though the interior was restored successfully under the management of informal community bodies, there are several challenges and threats for the mosque. Kosaituli was originally a low density area. Over the last few decades, the Muslim population has increased significantly in the local community and surrounding areas. As the capacity of the original mosque structure is about one hundred only, a four story extension block had to be added to the east to accommodate the increasing number of worshippers. This extension, though unavoidable for the continuity of the functioning of the mosque, remains a major threat to the heritage mosque. Replicating the original *Chini-tikri* was not possible (for lack of funding) in the extension; the appearance of the mosque was significantly disturbed.

Over the issue of the new extension and restoration of the mosque, there has been few disagreements between the newly selected mosque committee members and former committee members recently. However, the issue was resolved amicably probably due to presence of greater social capital. The most serious threat to the future of the heritage mosque (and other similar structures) has been the ever decreasing number of specialist *Chini-tikri* craftsmen. Of the few remaining senior master craftsmen, several have died of natural aging. The remaining few may not be able to support the craft for too long as many are shifting to other professions for lack of job. Several members of the mosque committee are concerned whether they will be able to find such quality master craftsmen (worked on the interior) who know the original style and can execute restoration of the exterior of the mosque.

FIGURE 5.9: Pogose High School
The Pogose school building exhibits some of the finest elements of British colonial architecture, showing nineteenth century detailing of wooden and iron beams, window shades, door louver and facade details.

Source: Author

POGOSE HIGH SCHOOL

Located on *Chittaranjan* Avenue at *Shankharibazar* of Old Dhaka, Pogose High School is the oldest school in the country that survives today. It was established in 1848 by N P Pogose, an influential Armenian merchant and *Zamindar* (feudal land owner), as the first private school in the region. The original school building exhibits some of the best elements of British colonial architecture (see Figure 5.1 and 5.9). Still privately owned and not included as a protected heritage by the government (even though it is more than 100 years old), the school has been functioning for about 163 years. The heritage building is managed by the Pogose school committee with occasional help from the *Shankharibazar Panchayet*.

Over the years, the number of students has increased significantly, which the original school building couldn't accommodate anymore. To maintain authenticity of the heritage building, the school committee decided to build new blocks within the large school compound. The school committee organizes repair/restoration of the heritage building during yearly school vacation. An annual survey is conducted by the committee during this period to detect areas where major repair/restoration work is required. *Shankharibazar Panchayet* supports the activity by supplying master craftsmen and skilled labors who are familiar with the construction style. As there has been regular maintenance, there has been no condensation on the surface or vegetation growth over the years. The heritage management activities are financed from school fund, formed through donations.

Due to growing age of the building, despite regular maintenance, a number of doors, windows, shades, louvers and especially original wooden beams supporting the roof became vulnerable to termite attack during the turn of the century. Greater funds (than usual yearly fund) were required to undertake the much needed restoration. Special donations were sought from parents, donors, patrons and local community members. As the school has a regular fund, the additional part of the fund could be managed over a few years. The next issue was finding expert master carpenters who knew the authentic style of woodwork of the building. The local Panchayet was particularly helpful in this issue; they also helped in organizing the fund collection. Finally, the major restoration work started in 2008 and took about two years to complete.

As the building was in use and well maintained, no details were entirely lost. During the restoration, special care was taken to maintain the original nineteenth century detailing of wooden and iron beams. Other parts restored were window shades, door louver and facade details. The significance of the restoration was the finance. Despite being one of the most renowned institutions and a heritage building, there was no government support for the restoration. The entire project was carried out with private funding and support of local community members. The restoration was co-managed by the school committee and *Shankharibazar Panchayet*. The case shows that for secular buildings, the community support system that grows on social capital has been equally successful in maintaining the authenticity of local heritage. Even though the restoration was done successfully, unplanned developments in the adjoining area remain a constant threat to the heritage. Another challenge is the limited school fund, which has to be prioritized for other uses. The two cases bring forward several key characteristics and activities (such as deliberation, decision making and fund raising) of heritage management in Old Dhaka. While not entirely similar, a

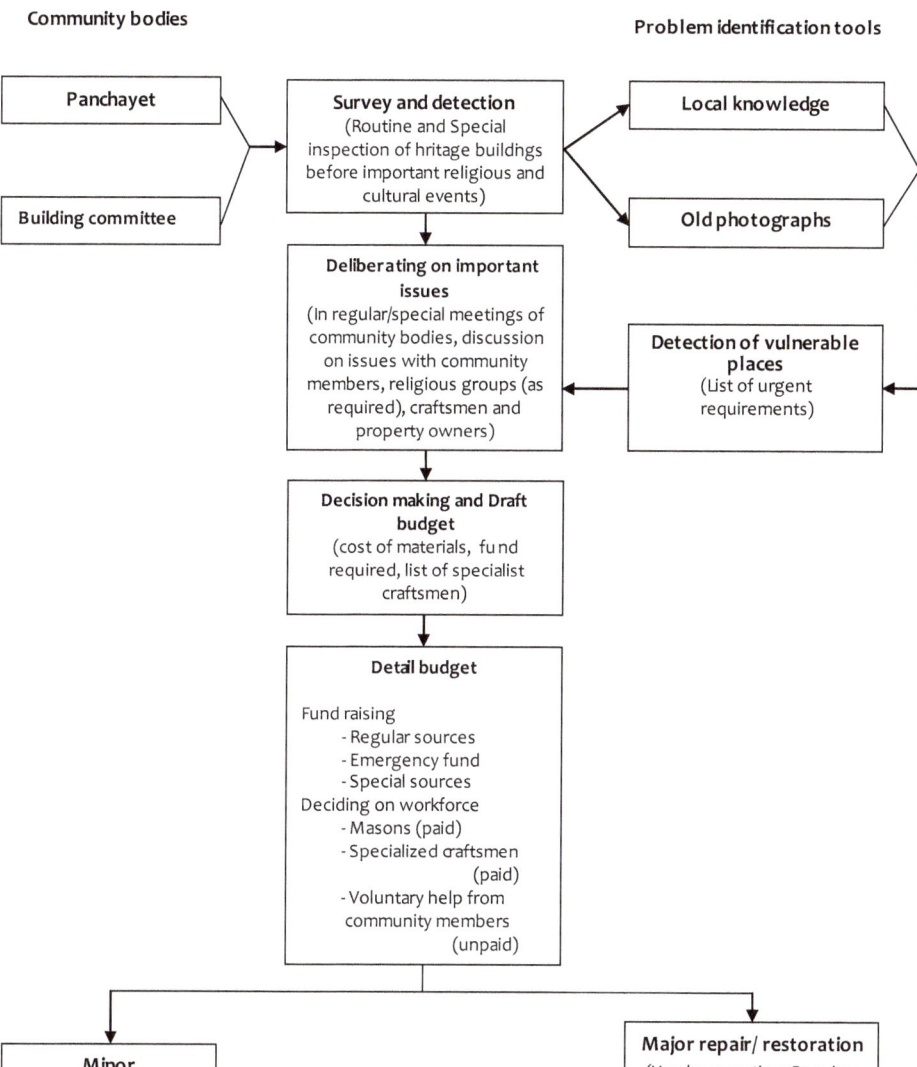

FIGURE 5.10: Summary of the informal heritage management activities in Old Dhaka

The figure shows important stages of the management process such as survey, deliberating, decision making, making budget and restoration, etc.

Source: Author

pattern can be identified. Figure 5.10 shows a summary of informal heritage management activities in Old Dhaka.

An integral part of the informal heritage management system is continuity of traditional construction methods and materials. The summary of activities of the two cases presented shows importance of the system of apprenticeship in Old Dhaka. Knowledge of local construction style, ornamentation and detailing are carried on by craftsmen and master builders through the system of apprenticeship. The survival of the apprenticeship depends on projects where a master craftsman can oversee a team of senior/junior apprentices in restoration work. In most heritage buildings, the original vernacular construction method of masonry and ornamentation has been maintained by the community based heritage management system till now.

The heritage management system in Old Dhaka involves multiple stakeholders; it is fostered by communities where social capital is strong and it is carried on by building owners, community bodies, community members, master builders and their apprentices. The decision making is participatory where informal community bodies, building committees and senior master craftsmen jointly decide the course of action before restoration. The heritage management system in Old Dhaka has been maintaining the local heritage till now, but it is struggling and faces several steep challenges for its survival in the rapidly changing urban environment.

FUTURE OF INFORMAL HERITAGE MANAGEMENT IN OLD DHAKA: CHALLENGES AND RECOMMENDATIONS

Two clear issues emerge from the study. First, the informal community bodies of Old Dhaka have been managing the local heritage despite limited resources, and it has been facilitated where there is a strong base of existing social capital. The shortage of funding has been compensated with community support and knowledge of vernacular construction methods. Second, there is no denying that with challenging economic conditions and transforming urban forces, managing the local heritage is getting tougher everyday and local communities need external support; either from government or NGOs. In several cases, the communities refrained from seeking external support (even though they direly need it) as they want to maintain 'community ownership' and they are afraid no formal intervention will consider this.

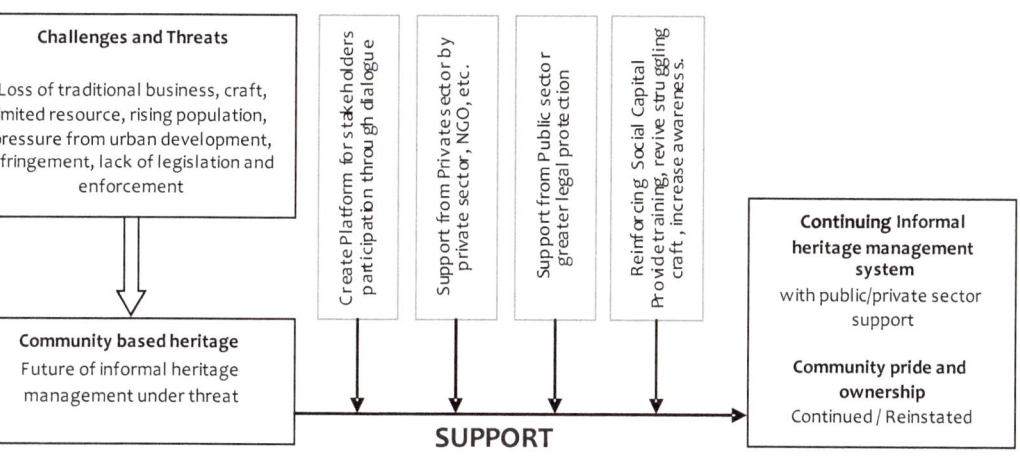

FIGURE 5.11: A possible support system for future of informal heritage management system in Old Dhaka
The possible components of a support system where both public and private sector needs to be involved in a limited capacity for the informal community bodies to continue with their heritage management.

Source: Author

Bangladesh has an existing system of NGOs working parallel to the government in urban areas. Generally, they fill the gap where government efforts fall short. The existing NGO infrastructure can be used to provide support to the informal community bodies of Old Dhaka to manage the heritage. However, external support must come with a better understanding of the informal heritage management system. This is crucial for any future support system with external stakeholders' involvement. For the communities to continue managing local heritage, there should be minimum influence on the existing informal heritage management system. A platform should be created for effective dialogue between external stakeholders (such as NGOs) and communities.

Figure 5.11 shows the challenges and threats against the heritage of Old Dhaka with possible components of a support system. It should be noted that both public and private sector needs to be involved in a limited capacity for the informal community bodies to continue with their heritage management. While short-term support may come in the form of arranging necessary financial support, long-term support should include better legislation, training in contemporary heritage conservation techniques, documentation of traditional knowledge, revival of struggling crafts, increasing awareness about local heritage, etc. With increased social activities in future, the support system will possibly enhance social capital in the traditional communities as well.

The existing heritage management system may be more effective with external support and structured empowerment. Empowerment should include fostering and enhancing already existing sense of ownership (of heritage) within the community and fostering a self-help approach to encourage voluntary contributions of labor and funding. Stakeholders should initially gather data on local heritage, arrange workshops, interviews, focus group discussions, etc. This should be followed by proper documentation of traditional knowledge. Department of Archaeology should work towards more effective legislations and should hire more skilled personnel in heritage conservation. For continuity of the informal heritage management system, NGOs should work as facilitators where they fill the gap where government efforts fall short. They should co-ordinate the external support and stakeholder involvement. However, any external stakeholder involvement must include the community in the overall conservation process. A delicate balance of power must be achieved.

CONCLUSION

With community participation in the conservation process, lost meanings are recovered, revived and re-established to assert the true spirit of place. No top-down/global policy can accommodate local community values. Conservation approach should be place-specific where traditional vernacular practice guides conservation decisions. People's participation should be active and spontaneous. Local crafts, spatial arrangements, traditional architectural forms and styles must continue for survival of heritage. Especially, local intangible heritage elements such as customs and traditions that are true to the place (both *living* and lost) deserve the highest attention.

In Old Dhaka, where the base of social capital is relatively stronger, the communities can come together, participation is more natural, community members have a greater capacity to solve problems. The two case studies clearly demonstrate that presence of greater social capital better facilitates collective action for heritage management governed by community bodies. Although the informal heritage management process shows promise, the system faces tough challenges such as financial restraint, dwindling or disappearing crafts, etc. Perhaps communities with substantial social capital can use it to better cope with these challenges than others. However, it is undeniable that they may not be able to continue without external support. Considering the local context, support comes with the risk of overpowering communities which they are aware of. This is a delicate situation that requires involvement and deliberation of all concerned stakeholders.

Leveraging existing social capital entails progressive reform of the existing system with a possible collaboration that has a delicate balance of power. The process must be inclusive where the local communities must have equal say in the process as they had. The stakeholders will be more complex when there is external support, the critical factor would be continuing to allow a broad cross-section of community members to have a voice in the community actions initiated in collaboration. Existing community networks need to facilitate support of external stakeholders; one should not restrict or overpower the other. Ultimately the ownership must remain with the community for survival of local heritage.

REFERENCES

- Ali, T. (2007, 16 April). Panamnagar Unscientific restoration defacing heritage. *The Daily Star.* Retrieved from www.thedailystar.net/2007/04/26/d7042601107.htm
- The Antiquities Act, Act No. XIV of 1968, amended 22 September 1976 Stat. (Peoples Republic of Bangladesh 1968).
- Azam, K. (1907). *The Panchayet System of Dhaka* (Reprint ed.). Dhaka: Asiatic Society of Bangladesh.
- Bagguley, P., Mark-Lawson, J., & Shapiro, D. (1990). *Restructuring: Place, Class and Gender.* London, UK: Sage Publications.
- Bonnici, U. M. (2005). The human right to the cultural heritage – The Faro Convention's contribution to the recognition and safeguarding of this human right. In C. o. Europe (Ed.), *The Faro Convention* (pp. 53). Faro: Council of Europe Publishing.
- Bourdieu, P. (1985). The Forms of Capital. In J. Richardson (Ed.), *Handbook of Theory and Research for the Sociology of Education* (pp. 241–258). New York: Greenwood.
- Cnaan, R. A., & Milofsky, C. (2007). *Handbook of Community Movements and Local Organizations*: Springer US.
- Coleman, J. S. (1988). Social Capital in the Creation of Human Capital. *American Journal of Sociology,* 94 (Supplement), S95-S119.

- Dani, A. H. (1956). *Dacca: a record of its changing fortunes.* Dacca: University of California
- Digital Globe [Software]. Redmond, WA: Microsoft Corporation. (2017). Available from https://zoom.earth/#23.709904,90.407009,16z,sat
- Dolff-Bonekämper, G. (2009). The social and spatial frameworks of heritage – What is new in the Faro Convention? In C. o. Europe (Ed.), *Heritage and beyond* (pp. 69-74). Paris, France.: Council of Europe Publishing.
- Council of Europe. (2005, 27 October 2005). The Faro Convention : Council of Europe Framework Convention on the Value of Cultural Heritage for Society. Paper presented at *The Faro Convention*, Faro.
- Flora, C. B., & Flora, J. L. (1993). Entrepreneurial Social Infrastructure: A Necessary Ingredient. *The Annals of the American Academy of Political and Social Science, 529*, 48-58.
- Fukuyama, F. (1995). *Trust: the social virtues and the creation of prosperity.* London, UK.: Hamish Hamilton.
- Imamuddin, A. H. (1982). Bengali house in urban context. *BUET Technical Journal*.
- IMF. (2013). *Bangladesh: Poverty Reduction Strategy Paper.* Asia and Pacific Dept: International Monetary Fund.
- Kilian, J. (2008). *Training and Education in Crafts for Conservation summary of outputs from CIF scientific working program 2005-2008.*
- Loury, G. (1977). A Dynamic Theory of Racial Income Differences. In P. Wallace & A. LaMond (Eds.), In *Women, Minorities, and Employment Discrimination* (pp. 153–188). MA: Heath: Lexington.
- Loury, G. (1992). The economics of discrimination: Getting to the core of the problem. *Harvard Journal for African American Public Policy, 1*, 91-110.
- Lowenthal, D. (1993). What makes the past matter? . In B. Farmer & H. J. Louw (Eds.), *Companion to Contemporary Architectural Thought* (pp. 182). London, New York. : Routledge.
- Mui, L. Y. e. a. (2008). Kuala Lumpur Georgetown as a Heritage City: The Voices of the Residents. Paper presented at *the 14th Pacific Rim Real Estate Society Conference*, Universiti Sains Malaysia.
- Per capita income now $1,180. (2014, 22 May). *Dhaka Tribune*. Retrieved from http://www.dhakatribune.com/bangladesh/2014/may/21/capita-income-now-1180
- Portes, A., & Sensenbrenner, J. (1993). Embeddedness and Immigration: Notes on the Social Determinants of Economic Action. *American Journal of Sociology, 98*, 1320-1350.
- Putnam, R. (1993). *Making Democracy Work: Civic Traditions in Modern Italy.* Princeton, NJ: Princeton University Press.
- Roy, M. K., & Sarker, G. C. (2006, April 26). Rural and urban Migration: The Role of Secondary Cities. *The Daily Bangladesh Observer*, p. 4.

- Taylor, J. (1840). *A sketch of the topography & statistics of Dacca.* Calcutta: Military Orphan Press.
- Taylor, M., & Singleton, S. (1993). The Communal Resource: Transaction costs and the Solution of Collective Action Problems. *Politics and Society, 21*, 195-214.
- UNESCO. (1996). *Cities of Asia: Heritage for the future.* Paris, France.: UNESCO World Heritage Centre.
- Winter, T., & Daly, P. (2012). Heritage in Asia: Converging forces, conflicting values. In P. Daly & T. Winter (Eds.), *Routledge handbook of heritage in Asia* (pp. 8). New York, USA. : Routledge.
- Wise, J. (1883). *History of Dhaka city* (Reprint ed.). Dhaka: Asiatic Society of Bangladesh.
- Woolcock, M. (1998). Social Capital and Economic Development: Towards a Theoretical Synthesis and Policy Framework. *Theory and Society, 27*, 151-208.
- WPR. (2016). Bangladesh Population 2015. from http://worldpopulationreview.com/countries/bangladesh-population/

FIGURE 6.1: The central mausoleum of Chhoto Katra crammed by illegal encroachment
The single dome mausoleum, almost forgotten now, sat on the center of the courtyard that acted similar to an urban plaza and most likely functioned as a bazaar with temporary stalls. The mausoleum was square in plan with corner turrets with a rectangular platform in the west. The extreme encroachment over the courtyard has completely shadowed the mausoleum.

Source: Author

A COMMUNITY-INVOLVED STRATEGIC MANAGEMENT PLAN FOR CHHOTO KATRA

Mohammad Habib Reza
Iftekhar Ahmed

INTRODUCTION

Caravanserai has a significant place as an integral part of trade routes in the medieval period; their presence indicates growth and prosperity of a city. Like other prominent Islamic empires, from the sultanate period onwards, caravanserais can be traced in major urban areas of Bengal, often as an informal structure. It was the Mughals who redefined caravanserais as formal structures in this region. Nearly all the rulers have left their imprint with caravanserais in their capital and regional states. Further, they marked major trade routes by building a series of caravanserais. Lost somewhere in the sands of time is a trade route (hardly traceable anymore) that linked Sonargaon with Delhi through Dhaka.

Seventeenth century Dhaka was a provincial Mughal capital that gained importance as a trade center due to the presence of the water-based transport system. Naturally, notable caravanserais were built in and around Dhaka. The caravanserais built in this region, locally known as Katra, have developed as a regional variant with their origin in the Ottoman and Mughal caravanserais. Katras provided traders a place to rest, discuss business, refresh for their next journey. Chhoto Katra is one of the two Katras built in Dhaka by the Mughals. During its hay day, Chhoto Katra along with Bara Katra was the center of trade and commerce of Mughal Dhaka.

Dhaka lost its prominence when the capital was transferred to Murshidabad in 1704 CE, so did the katras. This was followed by a subsequent abandonment till the early days of the British colonial period, converted to a school afterwards. Taken over by the Mughal descendants and illegal occupants subsequently, who freely altered and modified the structure, the heritage property fell victim of rapid urbanization, lack of awareness, improper conservation initiatives and currently in a state of decay where it's really hard to trace back to the original state. Though it was included as one of the 93 protected heritage buildings by the government, previous attempts to recover the heritage property failed due to the ambiguous ownership pattern and incompatible government policy. This chapter aims to identify the risks and threats that Chhoto Katra faces, reviews compatibility of the existing conservation legislations and finally recommends a strategic management plan suggesting possible local community involvement.

SOCIOPOLITICAL CONTEXT

Dhaka became a provincial Mughal capital in 1608 CE and was renamed *Jahangirnagar* after Jahangir. With its river transport, the city achieved great commercial importance as a center of the world-wide muslin trade and became a prominent trading center in the South to South-East Asia (Ahmed, 2012; Karim, 1964). In addition, it was an important junction in the trade route (hardly traceable anymore) that linked Sonargaon with Delhi. European traders from several countries started to come and many, especially the early Armenians, settled in the city. More European settlers came during the late seventeenth century, mainly consisting of the Portuguese, Dutch, English and French traders. Dhaka was noted as a remarkable international entity during Shaista Khan (1662–1689 CE), the city expanded to a population of a million people and measured nearly 20 by 13 kilometers (Karim, 1991). The city started on the northern bank of the river Buriganga and expanded towards north. During this period, *Chawkbazaar, Karwanbazaar, Farashganj* became bustling

FIGURE 6.2: Buriganga riverbank in 1861 CE
Charles D'Oyly's sketch shows Chhoto Katra held an important place in the cityscape suggesting its prominence.

Source: British Library Online

business centers, especially the places near the river turned into the center of all activities. These places were junctions where people came for business, recreation, religious and administrative purposes. They were housed in structures such as forts, palaces, mosques, temples, katras, row houses, etc. (Dani, 1961; Hasan, 1983). Later sketches (see Figure 6.2) of the riverbank show prominent Mughal characters such as, arch, minarets and domes (8 sketches of Dhaka river front, 1817).

As the sketch shows, katras held an important place in the cityscape suggesting their prominence. It can be simply assumed that during the Mughal era river played a vital role in international trade and intercity connectivity. Katras acted as selected portals that connected urban centers with the river.

IMPORTANCE AS CARAVANSERAI AND PRESENCE OF TRADE ROUTE

Serai is a Persian word meaning a halting place. The caravanserai form is believed to have Persian origins. However there is debate about the origin of its form, but it is generally considered that the inspiration came from either palaces or *vihāras*[1] (Sims, 1978). Nevertheless, the various adapted forms of caravanserais show the presence of both influences. Caravanserai was a place to rest for travelers/traders, discuss business, refresh for their next journey; it provided overnight accommodation with their pack animals and generally consisted an enclosed yard with chambers around. To accommodate these functions, caravanserai was designed as a fortified structure with a central courtyard and a cellular growth of rooms all around it, the number and size widely varying with the significance of its location within a city or trade route. Generally, its form was either square or rectangular in plan, concentric in nature, with or without bastions marking the fortification wall and towers at the angles. The access was often through a single portal placed at a location on

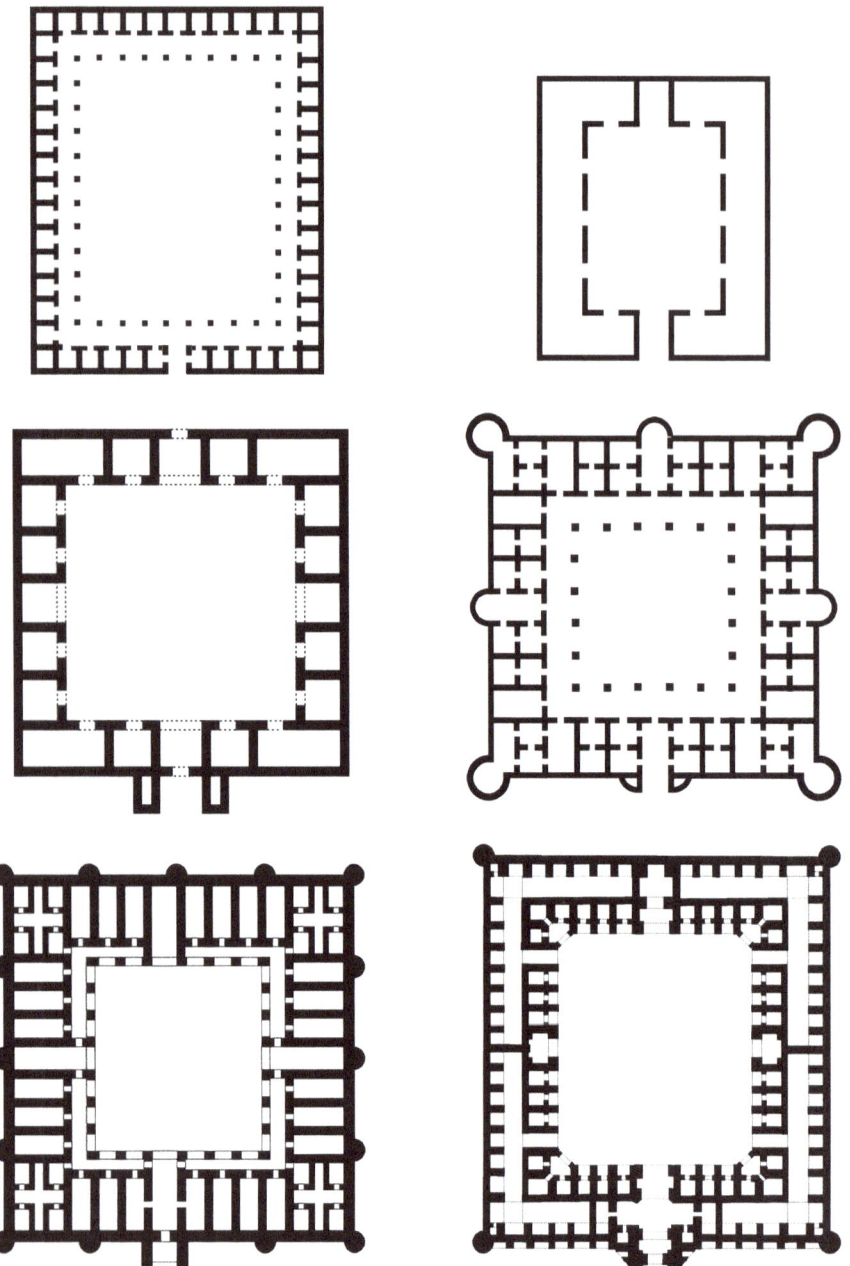

FIGURE 6.3: A variety of caravanserais and related buildings
The various adapted forms of caravanserais show presence of both Persian and Indian influences. Caravanserai was a place to rest for travelers/traders, discuss business, refresh for their next journey; it provided overnight accommodation with their pack animals and generally consisted an enclosed yard with chambers around.

Source: Author

the orthogonal axis. Often, the courtyard of the caravanserai was surrounded by arcades, with emphasis at the central bays, following the traditional four *iwan*. Toilets were placed in the towers at the corners of the building. In later caravanserais, an extra zone between the living quarters and the peripheral wall was developed to house stables for the animals (Pope, 1971).

Even though caravansaries existed in the Indian subcontinent before the Mughals, its form and typology flourished during the Mughal era. Based on form and functional attributes, they can be broadly categorized into four (Khan, 1990) or five (Dar, 2000) forms, respectively (see Figure 6.3). The most common form of Mughal caravanserais in the Indian subcontinent are the wayside serais. Generally located along highways between large city centers, they typically have two gateways with enlarged corner rooms. There was usually a bazaar, a mosque, and a well within these serais. Fort-cum-serais, the second type, developed during the early sixteenth century CE to provide overnight accommodation with protection. They generally have a single gateway and four solid corner bastions. The exterior walls have parapets on the top with space for soldiers to defend the structure. The third type, mausoleum-cum-garden serais, developed during the Mughal era. As their name suggests, generally they were located within the proximity of a garden or mausoleum and were most likely to be urban. Most of them have mosques and four-*iwan* arrangements with internal water sources. Town serais, a possible equivalent of modern hotels, had facilities such as public *hammam*, different types of eateries, etc. They were commonly located close to city gateways, near the main market and/or important parts of urban centers. The last category is custom-clearing serais, probably the most prominent one, had double compounds with one larger than the other. The traders entered the larger compound through the first gateway and waited to be allowed to pass into the adjoining smaller compound for custom clearing. Once cleared, the traders left through the second gateway (Campbell, 2011).

The caravanserais built in Bengal, locally known as Katra, have developed as a regional variety of the Mughal caravansaries. Boro Katra, one of the two surviving caravansaries of eastern Bengal, was most probably served as a custom-clearing serai. Chhoto Katra, the other one, has a layout and position in Dhaka during its days as the Mughal provincial capital that strongly resembles that of a town serai. However, it's a unique regional hybrid variety that adapted the forms of fort-cum-serais, mausoleum-cum-garden serais and town serai.

FIGURE 6.4: Charles D'Oyly's sketch of Chhoto Katra
The sketch shows Chhoto Katra during the early eighteenth century with the four-iwan arrangement with a mausoleum at the center.

Source: Drawing by D'Oyly (D'Oyly, 1817)

Charles D'Oyly's sketch (see Figure 6.4) of early eighteenth century (D'Oyly, 1817) shows the four-*iwan* arrangement with a mausoleum in the center.

The Katra is rectangular in plan, 334 feet × 304 feet externally and 268 feet × 228 feet internally (see Figure 6.8). The two storied southern gateway was the main entrance with four corner turrets with a fairly wide wooden stairway. East, west and the southern wings, except the gateway, was single storied. There were two octagonal chambers at the outer corners of the southern wall. The single dome mausoleum sat in the center of the courtyard was square in plan with corner turrets with a rectangular platform in the west. The *iwans* at eastern and western wing were projected towards the courtyards. The north wing was double storied, probably the upper story was a later addition. The courtyard acted similar to an urban plaza and most likely functioned as a bazaar with temporary stalls. As per Mughal tradition, the mausoleum platform was perhaps used for cultural performances.

Once the Mughal provincial capital was shifted to Murshidabad, for about hundred years, the Katra was adapted to various types of uses. Ultimately, the discontinuity of its original use led to various phases of illegal occupations resulting in decay and improper modifications of the structure.

DISCONTINUITY OF FUNCTION AND PRESENT STATE

Before the Mughals, Bengal was governed by different Muslim sultans of Turks and Pathan origins from 1204 to 1608 CE (Eaton, 1993). Arguably Dhaka and its surrounding areas were an urbanized settlement since seventh century CE based on its explored antiquity (Nilufar, 2010); and according to the popular belief, it had *fifty-two bazars and fifty-three lanes* with its center near the river. During this period, *Chawkbazaar* became a prominent trade center as it was located in front of the Afghan fort (former Dhaka central jail), which was the administrative center. After Shah Shuja (1639–1660 CE) was appointed as Mughal Subedar of Bengal, he identified the importance of the area and positioned Bara Katra, the first caravanserai, on the river bank in 1643 CE (Begum, 2015). Next two decades saw Dhaka flourishing and when Shaista Khan was appointed as the Subedar of Bengal (1663 CE) he felt the necessity for another caravanserai, different in nature than the Bara Katra which was used as a custom-clearing serai (see Figure 6.5). In 1664 CE, he built or rebuilt Chhoto

FIGURE 6.5: Chhoto Katra and its surroundings in map of Mughal Dhaka
Dhaka and its surrounding areas were an urbanized settlement since seventh century CE based on its explored antiquity; and according to popular belief it had fifty-two bazars and fifty-three lanes with its center near the river.

Source: Dani (Dani, 1961)

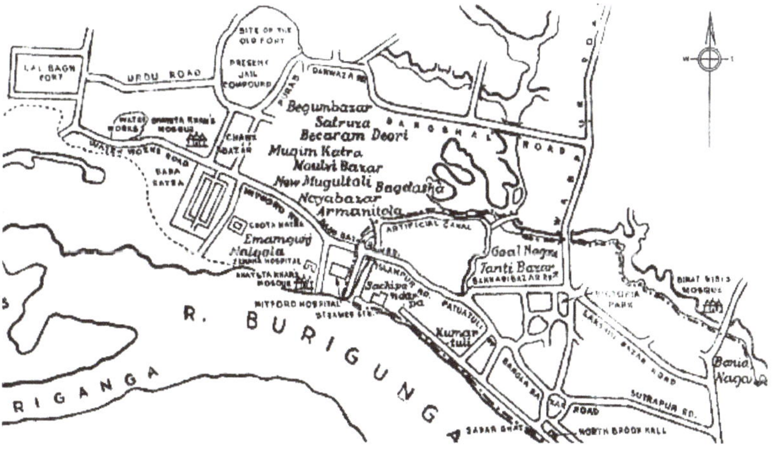

Katra (Taifoor, 1965) as a town serai in its vicinity (about 200 yards east of the complex) as a supporting facility which later evolved to support other activities.

Chhoto Katra continued to thrive till the end of Shaista Khan's reign in 1688 CE and was actively used as it was originally intended. It can be rationally assumed that it continued to be used as a caravanserai till the early eighteenth century CE when the capital of Bengal was shifted to Murshidabad. However, the gradual shift of city center towards northeast started earlier with the construction of the Lalbagh fort in 1678 CE by Muhammad Azam, son of Mughal emperor Aurangazeb. This shift probably acted as catalyst in the decline of Chhoto Katra, and finally stopped being used as a caravanserai after the British took over the Bengal in 1757 CE.

(a)

FIGURE 6.6: Chhoto Katra and its surroundings in 1859 CE
A second entrance connected Katra with Chawkbazaar as river-based trade became less significant with the rise of land-based trade during the British colonial period.

Source: Davey (Davey, 1863)

It can be further assumed that during the decline of Chhoto Katra, maintenance was irregular and subsequently several earthquakes hit this region[2] which may have contributed in its partial collapse. For about half a century or more Chhoto Katra remained abandoned, the

(b) (c)

FIGURE 6.7: Three development phases of Chhoto Katra and its surroundings
(a) CS Map of Dhaka 1912-15 CE
(b) RS Map of Dhaka 1953 CE
(c) Mouza Map of Dhaka 1989 CE

Source: (a) & (b) Land Record and Survey Department, Bangladesh
(c) M. S. Ali (Ali, 1989)

precinct was reused at the beginning of nineteenth century CE when it housed the first English Medium School in Dhaka (1816 CE) set up by Padre Leonardo. It was later converted as a branch of the French Normal school in 1857 CE (Mamoon, 1993). Most probably the British found the northwestern part partially collapsed and they added a second gate there providing access from the city (see Figure 6.6). As the river entrance (the main gate) lost its significance with the rise of land-based trade, the second entrance connected Katra with Chawkbazaar. At that stage the British probably altered some portion of Katra to fit their necessity. In 1864 Dhaka Municipality was formed which suggests the city was redeveloping and generating new urban activities. Later at some point normal school changed its mode and evolved as a primary teachers' training institutes, and became extinct at the first half of the twentieth century (Chwodhury, 2015).

Since the early twentieth century, Dhaka was redeveloping at a comparatively faster pace, and this part of the city had gained a greater density. Morphology of the neighborhood fabric shows Chhoto Katra lost its significance and it was not considered important enough to be protected. Next few decades saw Chhoto Katra getting engulfed with undesirable structures around and within its premise (see Figure 6.7a, 6.7b and 6.7c). Mughal descendants continued to

FIGURE 6.8: Chhoto Katra and its surroundings
(a) Chhoto Katra shown in satellite view
(b) Chhoto Katra shown in Mouza Map of Lalbagh, Dhaka 2004 CE

Source: (a) Digital Globe, 2017 & (b) Land Record and Survey Department, Bangladesh

occupy the premise in the decaying days of the structure, though their claim to be descendants cannot be verified. Furthermore, taking advantage of the unsettled ownership, there has been several illegal encroachments that overwhelmed the structure, making it impossible to distinguish between the original and later modifications. The road (built later) connecting the Katra gateways provides easy access to the illegal encroachers to occupy the central courtyard. Starting with temporary structures, the court was occupied to the extent that now the former open courtyard resembles a dense urban fabric (see Figure 6.8a and 6.8b).

As its typology suggests, the Chhoto Katra was positioned in the commercial heart of the city. The area retained its character, even after the Katra was not used as per its original function any more. Being a busy part of the city center, land value of this area continued to be high. To beat the competition for a place, the semi-abandoned state of the Katra offered illegal encroachers an easy target. Similar to shop-houses, local people are used to live near their business places (see Figure 6.1 & 6.9). This led to a two staged encroachment; first establishing the business place mostly occupying the rooms of the Katra, followed by making informal residences over the original structure, or in the courtyard. In most cases the makeshift structures were gradually replaced by permanent ones. It is common that a particular group of artisans or craftsmen created their enclave in

FIGURE 6.9: Present state of Chhoto Katra
The Chhoto Katra compound houses a variety of trade activities today and the modifications or alterations are highly chaotic. The original structure has undergone several stages of alteration, reconstruction and repair. During the last few decades, parts of Katra has been replaced with new structures.

Source: Author & Studio ARC 401 - Spring 2015, BRAC University

most traditional neighborhoods of old Dhaka. As the encroachment of Katra was gradual, taking place over the period of about a century, there is no fixed user pattern rather the business simply followed the market demand. As a result, the compound houses a variety of trade activities today and the modifications or alterations are highly chaotic. Amidst this chaotic development, the original structure has undergone several stages of alteration, reconstruction and repair. During the last few decades, parts of Katra has been replaced with new structures, that completely/ partially changed the Mughal appearance.

RISKS AND THREATS

In the local context, significant heritages rarely get the proper conservation efforts it deserves or they disappear into oblivion. Only a few of them get selected to be conserved either based on people's traditional belief as being *important* or archaeologists identify them as significant. Even the ones noticed as important enough are not always conserved or protected. Unfortunately, Chhoto Katra falls under this special category where it has been officially recognized as a significant monument, but there has been lack of any effort to conserve it. Even though it has been recognized as a monument worth protecting, the current framework of formal heritage conservation fails to protect due to multiple limitations.

(A) LIMITATIONS OF FORMAL HERITAGE CONSERVATION

The Department of Archaeology (DoA) of the Government of Bangladesh is responsible for preservation and protection of archaeological and heritage sites. Their activities are governed by the Antiquities Act, 1968, which replaced the Ancient Monuments Preservation Act, 1904 and the Antiquities (Export Control) Act, 1947. The legislation was enacted when Bangladesh was part of Pakistan, as East Pakistan. Despite the significant socioeconomic and political changes that have taken place after the country's independence from Pakistan in 1971, only one amendment was done in 1976. Till now the act is continuing to govern the country's heritage-related activities.

According to the prevailing Act, 'antiquities' is defined as any ancient (the preceding hundred years) product, object or site of historical, ethnographical, anthropological, military, scientific interest or declared by the Government to be an antiquity (Bangladesh, 1968). DoA is responsible for listing these antiquities as protected. In 2009 the DoA listed 93 heritage buildings and 7 heritage sites as protected by a gazette (RAJUK, 2009). Evidently this list represents only a fragment of the large number of heritage buildings and sites that needs to be protected. Also, there have been long running debates on whether a product, object or site should be considered an antiquity only based on time. However, at least in theory the gazette prohibits any demolition, amendment, selling or modification of these structures.

In addition to the local legislation, international charter such as the Athens Charter for the Restoration of Historic Monuments 1931 and the International Charter for the Conservation and Restoration of Monuments and Sites (the Venice Charter 1964) are referred in selective cases. The Athens charter adopted a seven points manifesto for restoration of historic monuments. One of them suggests to protect the surrounding of the historic sites, which is commonly interpreted as providing a buffer area of 250 meters around the site. Whereas, there has been several notable charters and conventions that supersedes these two charters and advocates many relevant issues [The Burra Charter-1999 (ICOMOS, 1999), The Nara Document on Authenticity-1994 (UNESCO, ICCROM, & ICOMOS, 1994), etc.]; unfortunately, DoA is not responsive to these contemporary ideas.

In addition, DoA has several limitations such as limited resources, inadequate personnel, complexity of heritage ownership, etc. Being a developing country, heritage conservation does not get serious attention from any government of Bangladesh. As such, DoA operates on a limited yearly budget highly inadequate to conserve/manage approximately few thousands monuments and heritage sites. This is also related to the number of professionals DoA can employ. As such, only a few selected heritage sites are prioritized for conservation and regular maintenance.

A group of untrained professionals, limited or without skills of conservation, has been involved in the selected projects of DoA till now. Recently few archaeologists have been recruited in the department who are in charge of supervising them. However, due to their inadequate number, the same group of untrained professionals is continuing to manage the heritage sites which often lead to inappropriate conservation decisions. Another major challenge for DoA is the complexity of heritage ownership and related land acquisition policies. In many cases DoA can acquire only part of the property and in others it fails to do so.

It is evident that the list of protected monuments and sites of 2009 only covers a small portion of the vast number of heritage sites that deserve to be protected. Many heritage sites fail to make it to the list either due to being considered not 'ancient' enough or there was an oversight in the field work. In case of the protected monuments and sites, the community loses the ownership to DoA. Due to DoA's limitations, the concerned personnel can rarely revisit the protected sites that ultimately leaves these sites virtually unprotected. In rare cases where the fund is available it comes with time limitation, this leads to hurried and improper conservation.

(B) DISTORTED HERITAGE PERCEPTION AND LACK OF COMMUNITY OWNERSHIP

As seen in old Dhaka, people living in and around Chhoto Katra use the premise both to live and work. It is evident from the previous discussion that they either illegally occupy the premise or they have unsettled ownership. Previous examples of similar cases show that government intervention generally eviction leads to without any rehabilitation. In case of a possible intervention, they fear not only to lose their place of living but also their livelihood. As a result, the local community actively resists any such possible government effort. This resistance is so fierce that even the DoA hasn't been able to conduct a proper physical survey of the premise yet.

There are several examples in old Dhaka where members of the community are proud of their heritage. This is partially absent here as many of the occupants are not aware of the significance of Chhoto Katra and there is vested personal interest. As the original use and glorious past of the monument is yet to be explored and disseminated to the public; occupants commonly perceive it as one of many old Mughal buildings of Dhaka. Again, many of them feel fortunate to have a property at such a lucrative location and they are in constant fear of losing it. Both of these factors act as a negative force against the possibility of forming some community pride about the monument.

In case of living heritage, generally there is a sense of belonging where the local communities feel that this is their own; often expressed in Bengali as *amader* (ours'). There are many examples where people form an informal community ownership where the heritage continues to be actively used. This is also related to community, the lineage of the heritage, where its stories are passed on to the next generations. In case of Chhoto Katra, unfortunately both are absent. As a result, there is absence of such community ownership which is a crucial element for any successful heritage management.

THE WAY FORWARD: STRATEGIC MANAGEMENT PLAN

Even though the idea of a strategic management plan is not new globally, many similar attempts have failed as top–down approaches were used. Especially since the nineties the importance of community participation has been recognized as an essential element for any successful heritage management. As already discussed, previous attempts of heritage management or even basic documentation was not successful due to resistance from the local community. Considering this reality, any future heritage management plan should include the local community as a principal stakeholder. In addition, as the original use and glorious past of the monument is yet to be explored, heritage documentation and dissemination should be the first step. The following process may be considered for a successful heritage management plan:

(I) RECOGNIZING COMMUNITY ISSUES

It is evident, there are a number of community issues that would directly or indirectly influence any possible strategic management plan. As such, the first step should be a survey consisting a number of questions to identify the characteristics and interests of the local community. The survey should focus on the following issues:

- Demographic characteristics of the area
- Social, economic and environmental challenges or priorities
- Identification of the property ownership pattern
- Backbone of community economic development

Local and international research and/or educational institutions may conduct the survey in collaboration with relevant government agencies such as DoA, Dhaka South City Corporation (DSCC), Rajdhani Unnayan Kartripakkha (RAJUK), Department of Land Records and Survey and Bangladesh Bureau of Statistics. Possible financing for the survey may come from international organizations, such as the World Bank, Asian Development Bank, UNESCO, AGA Khan Trust of Development, etc.

(II) IDENTIFYING HERITAGE VALUE

The previous discussion has established that the monument's history is obscure till date due to fragmented documentation. As a result, the heritage value of the monument hasn't been identified and the second step should be identifying it. The following issues need to be explored to establish the heritage value:

- A research dedicated to the history and characteristics of old Dhaka as its context
- A research dedicated to the history of the monument and surroundings to establish the timeline
- Identifying intangible heritage
- A complete documentation of the property

- Prepare the description, history, condition and integrity statements related to the heritage
- Describe the heritage values
- Preparing a dossier to potentially include the monument in international heritage lists

(III) INVOLVING RELEVANT STAKEHOLDERS

The current practice of heritage management in Bangladesh is highly top-down, where affected communities are ignored in the decision making process. For an effective heritage management plan, all relevant stakeholders, including the local community should be involved from the preliminary stages. It should be noted here the local community includes affected peoples within and surrounding the heritage site. To identify the stakeholders between them the first step should be recognizing (from the survey already conducted) different groups among the affected community. The second step is to decide the degree to which they are affected and their potential level of involvement in the heritage management process.

The next level will be involving relevant external stakeholders such as, Land Records and Survey and Bangladesh Bureau of Statistics in matters related to deciding property ownership pattern, Rajdhani Unnayan Kartripakkha (RAJUK) as the city development authority in matters related to deciding the proposed project's position in the overall city's development scheme, etc. The next group of stakeholders should play the role of facilitators and where applicable act as a party to incorporate the national and international interests, such as DoA, local NGOs and international bodies. After that, another set of stakeholders, such as academic/ researchers, who can potentially contribute with their specific field of expertise should be involved.

(IV) INITIATING POLICY CHANGE

There is a common misconception among the people involved in heritage management, possibly from a misinterpretation of the Athens charter, that every heritage site should have a buffer area of 250 meters around the site. Furthermore, there has been a recent initiative from the government to ban structures within 500 meters of protected heritage sites in Dhaka and within 1000 meters in the countryside. Previous discussion shows that the present government policy, including the misconception, needs to be reexamined and a new set of policy should be formed.

As most of the heritage sites are located amidst high-density urban fabric, any development process should include the local community from the early stages of policy formation with special focus on avoiding any possible gentrification. In similar cases, current practice shows that either the government has taken over the property removing local communities or simply there is an oversight, and the property is ignored continues to be managed by the local community. In such cases there is a possibility to introduce the concept of quasi-property where some rights similar to ownership may go to the local stakeholders who will act for the benefit of the heritage.

(V) INCLUDING THE PUBLIC

There is a possibility, if the proposed heritage management plan could be enforced, the Katra will be a proud national heritage and potentially attract a wide range of local and international tourists. Accepting the common people of the nation as a stakeholder, the initial draft of the heritage management plan should be shared with them. This can be achieved in two stages: firstly, disseminating the explored heritage value of the monument through various media such as newspaper, television, posters, websites, etc. This should be followed by organizing charrettes where selected public groups will participate and share their views about the future of the heritage.

FINAL THOUGHTS

At policy level the government of Bangladesh identifies the importance of heritage conservation as a significant sector of cultural development in the Seventh Five-year Plan (FY2016–2020). However, with a challenging economic condition the government has to prioritize among various sectors. As a common practice, heritage conservation and management is often a low priority sector in resource allocation. The above-mentioned heritage management plan has to be potentially executed under these constraints. The approach discussed here requires a gradual but essential change in government's way of thinking. On the other hand, the success of this community-led management plan will depend on the balance between personal and greater community interests in a shared platform where critical decisions have to be made collectively. In addition, several steps of the management plan may need to be improvised depending on the actual condition during the implementation phase.

ENDNOTES

1. Various forms of caravanserai show a resemblance with Buddhist *vihāra* (monastery). It is evident that there was strong connection between Buddhism and Persian culture (Foltz, 2010) during the earlier phase of Buddhist evolution at *Gandhara*. The Kusana period saw *Gandhara* become the regional cultural capital and an important junction of Indo-Persian trade route. A school of thought infers that early Persian caravanserais had been influenced by the early *vihāras* of *Gandhara*, especially Kusana form.
2. Several strong earthquakes hit Assam and Bengal in 1697, 1714 and 1759 CE (Iyengar, Sharma, & Siddiqui, 1999)

REFERENCES

- 8 sketches of Dhaka river front. (1817) (pp. plate 9). London: British Library.
- Ahmad, S., & Chase, S. C. (2004). Design generation of the central Asian caravanserai. Paper presented at the *1st ASCAAD International Conference*, e-Design in Architecture, Dhahran, Saudi Arabia.
- Ahmed, I. (2012). *A study of architectural heritage management by the informal community bodies in traditional neighborhoods of old Dhaka.* (Doctor of Philosophy), National University of Singapore, Singapore.
- Ali, M. S. (Cartographer) (1989). Mouza map of Lalbagh, Dhaka.
- The Antiquities Act (amended 1976) (1968).
- Begum, A. (2015). Bara Katra. In S. Islam & A. J. Ahmed (Eds.), *Banglapedia* (1 ed.). Dhaka: Asiatic Society of Bangladesh.
- Campbell, J. L. (2011). *Architecture and Identity: The Occupation, Use, and Reuse of Mughal Caravanserais.* (Doctor of Philosophy), University of Toronto, Toronto. Retrieved from https://tspace.library.utoronto.ca/bitstream/1807/29675/1/Campbell_Jennifer_L_201106_PhD_thesis.pdf
- Chwodhury, M. Q. (2015). Normal School. In S. Islam & A. J. Ahmed (Eds.), *Banglapedia* (1 ed.). Dhaka: Asiatic Society of Bangladesh.
- D'Oyly, C. (1817). *Antiquities of Dacca* (pp. plate 9). London: British Library.
- Dani, A. H. (1961). *Muslim Architecture in Bengal*: Asiatic Society of Pakistan.
- Dar, S. R. (2000). Caravanserais along the Grand Trunk Road in Pakistan–A Central Asian Legacy. *The Silk Roads: Highways of Culture and Commerce.*
- Davey, N. T. (Cartographer) (1863). City of Dhaka: Including cantonments.
- Land Record and Survey Department, Bangladesh (2004). Mouza map of Lalbagh.

- Eaton, R. M. (1993). *The Rise of Islam and the Bengal Frontier, 1204–1760*. Berkeley: University of California Press.
- Foltz, R. (2010). Buddhism in the Iranian World. *The Muslim World*, 10, 204–214.
- Hasan, S. M. (1983). *Glimpses of Muslim Art and Architecture*. Dhaka: Islamic Foundation.
- ICOMOS, A. (1999). *The Burra Charter (Charter for Places of Cultural Significance)*. Australia: Australia ICOMOS Inc.
- Iyengar, R. N., Sharma, D., & Siddiqui, J. M. (1999). Earthquake history of India in medieval times. *Indian Journal of History of Science*, 34(3), 181–237.
- Karim, A. (1964). *Dacca: the Mughal capital*: Asiatic Society of Pakistan.
- Karim, A. (1991). Origin and Development of Mughal Dhaka. In S. U. Ahmed (Ed.), *Dhaka Past Present and Future*. Dhaka: Asiatic Society of Bangladesh.
- Khan, I. A. (1990). The Karwansarays of Mughal India: A Study of Surviving Structures. *Indian Historical Review*, 14(1-2), 111–137.
- Mamoon, M. (1993). *Dhaka Smriti-Bismritir Nogori*. Dhaka: Anannya.
- Nilufar, F. (2010). *Urban morphology of Dhaka city: Spatial dynamics of growing city and the urban core*. Paper presented at the International Seminar on the Celebration of.
- Pope, A. U. (1971). *Introducing Persian Architecture*: Oxford University Press.
- RAJUK. (2009). *List of protected monuments and sites of Dhaka*. Dhaka: Bangladesh Gazette.
- Sims, E. (1978). Trade and travel: Markets and caravanserais. In G. Michell (Ed.), *Architecture of the Islamic world: Its History and Social Meaning*. London: Thames & Hudson Ltd.
- Taifoor, S. M. (1965). *Glimpses of Old Dhaka: A short historical narration of East Bengal and Assam*: S. M. Perwez.
- UNESCO, ICCROM, & ICOMOS. (1994). *The Nara Document on Authenticity (Nara Conference on Authenticity in Relation to the World Heritage Convention)*. Nara, Japan: UNESCO, ICCROM and ICOMOS.

www.ingramcontent.com/pod-product-compliance
Lightning Source LLC
Chambersburg PA
CBHW041431300426
44116CB00001B/6